Find a Way to Win

Management Insights from Terry Michler, America's All-Time Winningest Soccer Coach

by

Dan Coughlin

Published by

WORLD CLASS COACHING

First Printing May, 2010

WORLD CLASS COACHING
3404 W 122 Terr
Leawood, KS 66209
(913) 402-0330

ISBN 978-0-9826880-0-7

Edited by Tom Mura

Cover Design by P2 Creative

Dedication from Terry Michler

To all of my former players
for allowing me to be a small part of their soccer careers
and for their dedication to the CBC Soccer Tradition.

Also, thanks to all those who have influenced
my development over the years,
with special thanks to my Dutch friends,
Jan Pruijn, Harry Jansen, and Theo Derks.

Dedication from Dan Coughlin

To my wonderful parents, Gene and Laura Coughlin,
my terrific soccer coaches,
Jim Nolan, Ebbie Dunn, and Dennis Grace,
and my great wife, Barb, daughter, Sarah, and son, Ben.

Table of Contents

Foreword

Teamwork.

It's a beautiful thing when a team pulls together and achieves a great success. It doesn't happen all the time because not every team has a great coach. *Find a Way to Win* explores the coaching methods of extraordinary coach Terry Michler and teaches us how to apply them in a very practical, useful way—on the field and at work.

At work, teams are critical. Traditional, hierarchical leadership has diminished and the focus is now on the leadership networks and teams that are taking its place. Leaders find they are on all different sorts of teams, including virtual teams, autonomous teams, cross-functional teams, and action-learning teams.

The dilemma many leaders face is how to build effective teams as the time available to build them is decreasing. Leaders are often challenged by the necessity of building teams in rapidly changing environments with limited resources.

Implementing any teambuilding process successfully requires the leader to assume the role of coach or facilitator and to fight the urge to be the "boss" of the project. Great improvement in teamwork will occur if team members develop their own behavioral change strategy rather than if the leader develops the strategy in a silo and imposes it on the team.

Another issue that is not often addressed is what to do when one team member is ruining the team. Like Terry Michler and Dan Coughlin suggest in *Find a Way to Win*, surround yourself with positive influences. I also suggest that one bad apple gives the entire team the opportunity to work on improving their behavior. If everyone chooses something to work on, the team member having the issues won't feel so singled out by the manager.

You can do a little Feed*forward* exercise with the following easy steps:

1) Team members can ask each other, "What can we do to help our team demonstrate effective teamwork?

2) Encourage team members to be positive and focused in their replies, and to listen, learn from, and express gratitude for the suggestions.

3) Then each team member can discuss what they've learned from the other team members.

4) Provide the ideas – as manager of the team – in a summary of all the suggestions you've heard.

5) Ask each person to commit to following up with their fellow team members.

6) Participate in the process yourself. Leading by example is a key factor in the success of any great teambuilding process.

These suggestions will help, but they are just the very tip of the iceberg when it comes to teambuilding.

Find a Way to Win provides great insights, practical methods, and wonderfully useful ideas that business managers and coaches alike can use in all different sorts of situations to build great teams. Read it and you'll know all the secrets to building an extraordinary team!

Marshall Goldsmith is a world-renowned executive coach and million-selling author of the *New York Times* best sellers, *MOJO* and *What Got You Here Won't Get You There.*

Introduction

Every once in a while a person finds what he or she was looking for from the most unexpected source. This book is the story of such an event.

Find a Way to Win is about achieving team excellence both in soccer and in business. For several years I searched for practical ideas groups could use to deliver great business performances. However, it wasn't until The Game that the crucial ingredients for great business teamwork started flooding toward me.

Through a series of completely unforeseen events I ended up across the table from Terry Michler, who has won more soccer games than any high school, college, or professional coach in U.S. history. Over a period of several months we discussed a wide variety of approaches he has used to improve group performance in his 39 years as the head soccer coach at CBC High School in St. Louis, Missouri.

During that time he won 809 games, six state championships, and six state second-place trophies. His teams have made it to the Final Four 16 times and been nationally ranked 10 times. He was named National Coach of the Year by the NSCAA (National Soccer Coaches Association of America) and also by StudentSportSoccer.com. And he still has a long way to go in his career.

Based on Terry Michler's soccer coaching methods, this book gives business managers practical ways to improve group performances. If you are a business manager who coaches youth soccer, played high school soccer, and/or likes learning from someone who has achieved the pinnacle of success, you will enjoy these down-to-earth ideas from Terry Michler.

More important than his number of victories are the ways in which Terry has guided his team for the past four decades. One of his favorite sayings to his team is, "Find a way to win." Those five words mean a lot, a whole lot.

"Find" means keep searching for ways to get better as a coach, as a player, and as a team in the offseason, during practices, and during a game.

"A way" means that it's not enough just to win a game. You have to have an approach to the game. In CBC's case that approach is based on the concept of "ball possession attacking soccer." This overarching idea is equally as powerful for businesses as you will see in the upcoming chapters.

"To win" means it's not enough to look good or play hard or follow a strategy. In the end you have to go for the win. That's what all the mental and physical effort is directed toward. It requires maintaining flexibility and making adjustments within your approach during a game and during a season.

A manager is a person who is responsible for the results of a group performance. Whether you are a business owner, CEO, sales manager, not-for-profit executive director, or the person responsible for the results of any group performance, you are a manager.

Since 1998 I have worked full-time with corporate teams as a management consultant and business keynote speaker. These groups included more than two dozen teams within McDonald's Corporation in over fifteen regions, each of which had 400-500 McDonald's restaurants. The groups consisted of franchisees, vice-presidents, and directors of operations, marketing, business research, and human resources. My average time with each team was 14 months.

My consulting work has also been with more than a dozen cross-functional teams within Marriott International, the sales team of the St. Louis Cardinals, three cross-functional teams within The Coca-Cola Company, the insurance group within Toyota Financial Services, the Marketing Leadership Council within Prudential Capital Group, and dozens of other teams in large, medium-size, and small businesses.

While observing managers for more than 3,000 hours as they conducted meetings, dealt with crises, and made difficult personnel decisions, I saw what created effective teamwork and what kept groups from being successful. Many times team members shared with me what they felt was effective and not effective in building a successful team.

In listening to Terry Michler explain his coaching methods I realized how useful his ideas can be for business managers. To broaden my understanding of his methods for building great teams I interviewed his long-time assistant coach, some of his former players, opposing coaches, and coaches from around the world who have mentored him and whom he has mentored.

I believe you will relate to Terry not because he's famous like a Super Bowl champion football coach, but rather because he will remind you of a high school coach you had or yourself as a youth sports coach. While there are a number of books about or by football coaches there has never been to the best of my knowledge a business management book based on the methods of a soccer coach in the United States.

The value of this book is not in the fame of the coach, but rather in the quality of his ideas and their practical application for you.

My purpose in studying Terry Michler's approach to building successful soccer teams is to identify powerful ideas from him and then offer suggestions on how you can use them to improve results with your business team. The management insights drawn from his work are explained in the format of one entire year in his role as the head soccer coach at CBC High School.

Good luck to you as you apply Terry Michler's practical wisdom toward building extraordinary teams in your organization.

Dan Coughlin
May 1, 2010
St. Louis, MO
www.thecoughlincompany.com

Chapter One

State Championship

The Game led to The Question.

In searching for powerful insights to improve group performance it's important to always stay open-minded to every possibility. On November 21, 2009, I took my eight-year-old son, Ben, to see the Missouri Class 3 Boys High School Soccer State Championship Game. I wanted him to see soccer played at a very high level. Little did I realize what was going to happen starting that night.

The game was won by the CBC Cadets 1-0, but much more importantly was the way they won. It was one of the single finest displays of soccer I've ever seen at any level including collegiate and professional games.

The CBC players displayed a relentless intensity of passing, attacking, moving without the ball, and winning the ball back for the entire eighty minutes. Every CBC player was in sync with each of his teammates. Their goalkeeper did not register a single save, nor did they give up any corner kicks for the entire game. Their opponent had beaten them twice earlier in the season, but in the championship game CBC was nearly flawless.

We sat in the first row and barely heard the players talking. They seemed to know where to go and what to do spontaneously. They had no wasted effort. It all resulted in a precise, attacking style of play where every player fulfilled his responsibilities offensively and defensively in a remarkable manner. It was like watching a world-class jazz ensemble performing at its highest level in front of an audience of 5200 people.

When I got home that night I sent a congratulatory e-mail to Terry Michler. He and I had met briefly 20 years earlier, and I just wanted to congratulate him on one of the most amazing group performances I had ever seen in athletics, business, or entertainment. I didn't think he remembered me, and I certainly didn't expect a reply.

…and then the magic started to happen.

He sent me an e-mail that said, "Thanks for the kind words. I enjoy what I do and I continue to learn more about what I need to do. The passion to learn is still there."

Those last seven words really caught my attention.

Let me repeat. Terry Michler has been coaching and teaching at CBC High School for 39 years. He has six state championships. He has won more games than any soccer coach at any level in the U.S. has ever won. Yet he still has the passion to learn how to be better at what he does.

That is when The Question hit me:

> **How did Terry Michler make such an extraordinary group performance happen in the state championship game and could his ideas be applied by groups in the business world?**

I wanted to learn every coaching nuance he used that created this amazing team effort. I read his book, *Dutch Total Football*, where he described the enormous influence that the Dutch coaching approach to soccer has had on him. He wrote that he had been to the Netherlands nine times in the past 12 years to study Dutch soccer.

He explained there are more people from Holland coaching national soccer teams than from any other country. As I read his book I realized that what he was describing about Dutch football was exactly what I saw happen in the state championship game. I had a hunch that his ideas might have tremendous implications for business managers.

10 days after the championship game Terry and I sat down for three hours to discuss in much greater detail his thoughts on how to generate great group performances. I then wrote up his ideas into an article. I tried to convert his comments into management insights that I hoped would be useful for business managers who like soccer.

That simple article was posted almost immediately on dozens of websites around the world, and we received e-mails from people in Australia, Scotland, Holland, Jamaica, South Africa, England, and all across the United States. Somehow we had hit a nerve with people who were business managers by day and youth soccer coaches by night. Thus, the idea for this book was born.

For the next five months, Terry and I exchanged countless e-mails and had another dozen face-to-face meetings to discuss his thoughts on building extraordinary teams.

Throughout the rest of this book, his ideas are explained in great detail along with insights from his assistant coach, former players, opposing coaches, and other colleagues. Take the ideas that resonate with you and apply them with your work team.

Dan Coughlin: Your 2009 state championship was one of the finest soccer games I've ever seen a team play at any level. Your team's performance was one of the greatest group performances I've ever seen in business, entertainment, or athletics. What did you say to your team after the game?

Terry Michler: Here's a portion of what I wrote to the team:

Boys, I want to thank you for the wonderful season and the beautiful final game. The final represented a culmination of everything that we did and everything that we were about this past season. It all came together in one glorious game where we demonstrated in so many ways why we are the champions.

Welcome to a very exclusive group. This is a group that has in common the successful completion of a desired goal that is shared by many, but achieved by a very few. The memories will never leave you, nor will they ever diminish. They are yours to treasure for the rest of your lives. Welcome also into the history of CBC Soccer and St. Louis High School Soccer. You have left a permanent and lasting mark that will be there forever.

You have stamped your greatness along with others of deserving status. People will applaud you for the result, but they should also applaud the process of what it took to reach that goal.

As a coach, I will always remember the final as a special moment because so much was riding on the outcome and so much came together to produce the all-time best game possible. When we met on Saturday morning to discuss the tactics for the game I had a good feeling that everyone shared in the idea and thought that it was the best way to play.

Part two was to play it on the field. It was as close to a perfect game as I could have ever imagined. But maybe more important to me was how maturely you approached and played the game. There were so many great efforts and wonderful plays that it seemed that the game was easy and fun for you even though it was a championship game played before 5,000 people.

We asked you to enjoy the moment, have fun, and do your best. That is just what you did and your performance was awesome. You played to a championship level and deserve to be recognized for the champions that you are. I am sad to see it all end, but could not be happier for the way that it ended. Every one of you is a special part of this success and everyone together made it happen. Thanks for the memories. I have truly been blessed to be able to be a part of this with you.

Management Insight

When you celebrate a great success with your team reinforce for them what it took to make the success a reality. Notice how Terry reinforces the importance of a shared vision and the process necessary to make the vision a reality. He's actually teaching the players the formula for generating success later in life.

Chapter Two

Team Banquet

Special results require special events.

Approximately seven weeks after a state championship, CBC holds a special off-campus banquet for the soccer team. During the banquet Terry Michler and his assistant coach, Tom Farishon, reflect on the season, provide comments on each player and team manager, and celebrate the successes of the team.

In business you might do the same thing at an annual meeting with all of your employees. This is a time to include families in a meaningful way, recognize great individual and group success, and set the stage for the upcoming year. In many ways this banquet is an opportunity to teach lessons that can last for many years.

Include Families

Coughlin: Why do you feel it's important to include families in the end-of-the-year banquet? In what ways do you involve families in the course of the season? What do you see as the positives that are created by involving families?

Michler: Families are an important part of any organization, and the more they are on your side, the better. I have been very fortunate to have a very positive parent support group. Some of the dads have played for me and maybe that helps. It's mostly the moms that really want to get behind this.

A few years ago I had one of the moms ask if they could make pre-game meals for the boys. That was great, and we still do it today. This year the moms made pre-game meals for the home games, helped with our out-of-town trip, packed lunches for the boys, and organized the banquet. I think it's great that they want to get that involved, and I have no problem with letting them do it.

Over the years I have realized the importance that the family provides to the player. The parents are as much into what's going on as the players themselves. It is exciting to see the enthusiasm that the parents bring to the season and that helps to motivate the player to do his best.

Our program is tradition-based. We have brothers and fathers and uncles who have played here before. The "extended" family of CBC Soccer is rather extensive and the interest never seems to dwindle. When I see people who have a CBC or CBC Soccer connection, they are always interested to know how the team is doing. They also always have a story ready to reminisce about, and that tells me how connected they still are to the program and how important that connection is to them.

As I said earlier, the parent group asked if they could "take over" the banquet this year. They did a marvelous job throughout the year, and I was certain that they would make the banquet very special. One less thing for me to worry about! This is their way of being part of the team and making a contribution.

Normally during the year I will not get overly involved with the parents. I know that they have their own vested interest in their son, and my interest is in the team and their son, but with more than 20 sons it's just not the same. Once the player has finished his playing career at CBC, I am very available to the parents and the dynamics are quite different then. I think everyone understands that and respects my position.

Here is an excerpt from Terry's letter to the parent group, which he sent to one parent for distribution to the others, after the 2009 Championship Banquet:

Please share this with all the parents as I want them all to know how much what they did meant to us and it really showed throughout the banquet. This team was deep with players, but also with caring and helpful parents.

As a coach, my primary focus is on the players and their readiness to play, but a big part of that comes from the support they receive at home from the parents. I want to say thanks to all the parents who helped you and to those who kept their boys going throughout the grind of the season. Everything makes a difference, good or bad. Fortunately for us this year it was all good, and in the end it really showed.

As the curtain has now officially come down on the 2009 season, we share the feeling that it was truly special in more ways than just winning the championship. It's amazing what happened in a short time. The bonding and friendships that occurred will last forever.

The games and the team were the platform, but the real work was being done in many different ways and in many different places. We had a harmony and chemistry on the field and within the team, but we also had it off the field in our "extended" team. In closing, please feel my deep appreciation for all that you did, every one of you.

In the word TEAM: Together Everyone Achieves More – we truly were a TEAM!!

Thanks,

Terry

Management Insight

Your employees have lives. Those lives include their families. Try to include families in special moments at work in whatever ways you can realistically do it. If they can't be at the event, perhaps you can videotape comments from the family members and show them at the awards banquet.

Review Lessons Learned and Celebrate Victories

Coughlin: How do you use the team banquet as a means to teach the players useful lessons and to celebrate the season?

Michler: From the team performance perspective, I like to recap the season, particularly the defining moments. Every season has its own story, and the banquet is a time when I can retell that story and highlight the key moments. When you are "in the moment" situations seem different than when you can look back on them at a later time.

It's like the different events are pieces of a puzzle. Once the season has ended you can see if and why the pieces came together into a good fit or were just a bit off. Seldom does an entire season ever run smoothly. There are disruptions of different kinds that always act as "bumps in the road." The key to a successful season is how you handle those moments and how well you recover from them.

To know that there was a "bad patch" in the season and to have been able to work through it gives confidence and reassurance that persistence and staying on task do have rewards. The retelling of a championship season obviously leaves everyone feeling enthused and satisfied. It is always a great story to tell, and everyone loves a happy ending.

The seasons that did not go very well are more difficult, but still must be handled in an honest and sensitive way. It is always good to point out certain situations and indicate how maybe a small detail made a big difference. Try to make it a learning experience where the players can take something positive out of the situation.

Management Insight

Use your big meetings as opportunities to teach. What lessons do you want to convey and what is the best way for you to get them across? Don't miss an opportunity to teach a powerful point that can improve the future.

Highlight Each Player

Coughlin: During the team banquet you took the time to describe the season in depth, and you invested several minutes in discussing each player, regardless of how much playing time he had. Why do you think it is important to talk about the season, the team, and each player with such detail?

Michler: I always feel it is important to make each player feel good about his contribution by making a few personal remarks about him at the end-of-the-year banquet. Everyone did something during the year that made them feel good about themselves, and I like to try to capture a moment or a characteristic that is unique to each player.

It is my way of acknowledging that what they did caught my eye. Obviously each player is very different, and so are their contributions. Nevertheless, it goes a long way when they hear the coach personalize their contribution. I want them to know that I noticed. That is a positive reinforcement to validate their participation and maybe even encourage them to do more in the future.

I expect a lot from my players and from my teams. The banquet gives me an opportunity to give something back to the players in the way of compliments. Whenever you say something good and positive to someone they will remember it for a long time.

The banquet is the last official time the team will be together so there is no better time to send them off on a good note feeling good about themselves and what they accomplished.

Coughlin: You also put together a binder for each player with articles, letters from parents and fans, and a description of each player. Why did you put so much effort into the binder?

Michler: For each championship season I present each player with a "scrapbook" of the year. It takes a lot of work, but the memories are there forever. I know that when I look back on my own playing career I still get excited as I recall certain games and re-read certain articles about the season.

I want a special season to last as long as possible so the little bit of time that I invest is a drop in the bucket compared to the lifetime of memories that are provided. It makes me feel good that I can do this for the players who gave so much to be successful and to represent our CBC Soccer Tradition in the best way possible. It's the least I can do for them.

Management Insight

Make sure that in the course of a year's time that every employee gets some public recognition. This could be as simple as recognizing people whose birthday was that month. When you talk about the person in front of other employees take a few minutes to say specific things about the person.

Be willing on special occasions to create special gifts that create memories for a lifetime such as a scrapbook filled with articles, comments from team members, and pictures of key moments.

Chapter Three

Off-season

Championship teams are formed in the off-season.

Coaches and players go their separate ways to reenergize, hone their individual skills, and prepare for the upcoming season. For the CBC soccer team there is a little more than eight months from the state championship game of one season to the opening practice of the preseason the following year. Those eight months are crucial in getting ready for the potential 33 games they will play during the season.

Business managers and employees don't have an extended off-season of several weeks or months. Their customers expect them to be there to serve them today and tomorrow and the day after that.

However, they need to make time to get away from their work in order to reenergize, hone their individual skills, and prepare for upcoming projects, unforeseen crises, and difficult decisions. These times consist of a few hours here and there during the week and a day or so each month.

As Terry and I discussed the different aspects of the off-season it became more and more obvious to me how critically important that time is for the future success of coaches, players, managers, and employees.

Set the Stage for Next Season

Coughlin: Once the regular season is over what is the first thing you do?

Michler: The 2008 season ended on a very tough note. We lost on our home field in the state playoffs and our "B" team lost unexpectedly in their playoffs on our home field. As coaches we wanted to have a meeting immediately with all of the players who would be trying out for the varsity the next year to make it clear that this is NOT what we are all about. We didn't want to wait until the end of the school year to have the meeting.

We knew we couldn't affect what had happened, but we also knew that we could affect the future and not let it happen again. We weren't angry with the players, but we wanted to let them know that ending the season this early was not what we wanted.

If you don't step in right away, then this sort of thing can get into people's heads and become a habit, the wrong kind of habit. I wanted to make it clear to everyone right away which players were going to be the leaders in 2009 and that everyone was expected to follow them and match their work ethic.

Three days after those losses Tom and I held a meeting with all of the players who would be trying out for the varsity team the next season. We explained in detail nine points for them to remember. They were as follows:

1. CBC Soccer Pride
    - Season-ending losses at home being shutout were not acceptable!!!
2. Ego vs Toughness
    - Lower the egos and raise the toughness (mental and physical).
3. Mental and Physical Toughness
    - Have the will to win, fight, and compete every day in practice and games!!!
    - Avoid taking stupid fouls, lazy fouls, or soft tackles.
    - The harder you work, the more invested you become. It is harder to give up!!

4. Soccer Intelligence

    - Anticipation (what might happen next) versus reaction (what does actually happen).
    - Anticipation will ALWAYS beat reaction!!!
    - See the play and the next play and think ahead of the opponent.
    - Tactical discipline – be where you should be at the right time making the right play.
    - There is a serious deficiency in our ability to play in a thinking way. We simply react!!

5. Juniors vs Sophomores

    - Juniors are very serious and hard-working. They will work hard to be good.
    - Sophomores seem to be soft and want to be good.
    - The juniors will be the leaders next year and it will be their way: serious and hard-working.

6. Constructive Criticism

    - Take comments from coaches as a means to improve.
    - Work through tough times. Don't expect everything to come easily.
    - Be open to correction and become better because of it.

7. Tradition

    - CBC Soccer is deep in tradition.
    - Tradition is what the past provides for the present and the future.
    - The past presents challenges for the present to carry on and build for the future.
    - You must work very hard to maintain tradition.

8. CBC average record per season

   - 20 wins and 5 losses is the average over the last 38 years.
   - That is just average. A "C" in the classroom is average.
   - It takes an awful lot just to be average in CBC Soccer.

9. Underdog vs Front-Runner

   - The underdog has fight and fear and lower expectations, thus less pressure.
   - The front-runner has higher expectations and more pressure.
   - There is a certain amount of experience and maturity needed to be a successful front-runner.
   - It is a swagger vs fight out of fear.
   - Combine them and you have the best of both.

Management Insight

When the results are unacceptable, have a meeting right away with your team. Go into that meeting prepared to explain the key points you want your group to focus on in order to improve performance and results.

Don't go in there angry. Go in there with specific, honest insights for the members of the group to think about.

Give Players Room to Breathe

Coughlin: After your season is over with do you go and watch your players when they compete with their various club teams?

Michler: No, I don't. The reason I don't is I want them to have their own space to develop as players. I also don't want to unfairly judge them. When they are playing for someone else they are being asked to do certain things, which might be different than what I would ask them to do.

Consequently, I may be thinking they made the wrong decision when in fact it is exactly what they have been asked to do. I leave them alone during the offseason. That's their time to work on their skills and get in as good of physical and mental condition as they can.

Management Insight

Let your employees have "off-season" opportunities during the flow of a work week. Encourage them to get away from you and everyone else connected to their work life so they can be by themselves.

This alone time can be extremely productive in terms of improving results over the long term. It allows the employee to clear his or head and really think about key issues and objectives.

Surround Yourself with Positive Influences

Coughlin: You encourage people to actively seek out and surround themselves with positive influences. Why do you think this is so important and what advice do you have on how to make it a reality?

Michler: When you are satisfied where you are, watch as the competition passes you by. If you are standing still, you are in essence falling back. In order to keep up you must keep moving forward. Positive influences come from a variety of sources that include people, books, and videos.

My strongest influences come from two sources: first, the Dutch coaches and their approach and mentality towards soccer, and second, successful coaches and teams in the world of soccer.

First, I'll explain the Dutch influence. I don't think anyone can argue against the success of the Dutch in their contribution to soccer on a world-wide basis, especially given the size of their country and their population.

Soccer is as important a national resource and export to them as is any other major product they possess and develop. Through their soccer educational system they produce players and coaches that can be found everywhere in the world. This is an on-going situation, not an on-and-off occasional thing. Due to their limitation in size and population they maximize their resources in the best way possible.

Their soccer education and youth development programs are studied the world over. People come to Holland to learn and observe soccer, and Holland sends people around the world to show and tell about soccer. There is more of a Dutch influence in world soccer than from any other nationality.

As a result of their giving of their knowledge and expertise, it forces them to stay "ahead of the game." They cannot afford complacency and arrogance as they would surely be passed by. They continually seek to improve themselves first and then share the "goods."

I have been a Dutch advocate since 1974 and over the years have gotten much closer to the direct contact and influences than I ever dreamed that I would.

To have been to Holland eight times, to be able to call upon internationally-recognized coaches and instructors, and to call them my friends, truly is a blessing and one that positively influences me in a way that nothing else could.

The other way I've surrounded myself with positive influences is to study the successful coaches and teams throughout the world by reading and viewing. There are always reasons for successes, and the more I pursue those reasons the closer I get to the bottom of why they are so successful.

In my case, the passion to learn and improve still burns within me. It is rewarding to me when I come across information that coincides with my own personal approach. It reinforces that I am on the right path.

Soccer changes over time just like every other activity. History gives us a perspective of the past, but the present challenges us in different ways.

To stay current with the trends is very important. To see the evolution of ideas and phases shows the progressions made over time, and the challenge is to be on the cutting edge of what the future will hold for us.

Management Insight

Who are the positive influences you are surrounding yourself with? Which individuals are you meeting with regularly, what books are you reading, what videos are you watching, and who are you observing?

Are you steadily improving your understanding of what it is that you want to be great at?

Improve Individual Performance

Coughlin: What does it take for an individual to become an extraordinary performer?

Michler: Motivation plays a big part. It's always best if the motivation is intrinsic where the players want to get better, but sometimes I have to provide some additional motivation for them. If I need to be with a player at every moment to motivate him, then that's a problem.

There comes a moment when the player is on his own. If he can't motivate himself, then he'll never be an extraordinary performer. Some players need constant reinforcement, and those players just aren't going to become extraordinary performers.

Intrinsic motivation is important because no player can be an extraordinary performer without having taken his technical skills to a very, very high level. To do that requires thousands of hours of practice with effective coaches over a period of 10 to 12 years. No player will be willing to do that if he is not motivated to improve, and most of that motivation has to come from within the player.

Management Insight

Are your employees intrinsically motivated, or do you have to provide constant motivation for them to perform? If you always have to be there for them to stay motivated, how will they create and deliver more value for the customers when you're not there?

If they are not intrinsically motivated, you may very well have the wrong group of employees.

Coughlin: Anders Ericsson, a professor of psychology at Florida State University, is one of the premier experts in the world on expert performance. After years of research he has landed on the concept of "deliberate practice" as the critical factor in developing great individual performers.

I call this "thought-filled practice" because it's the type of practice where the performer is thinking about what he or she is doing before, during, and after the activity. I summarize his process of sustaining thought-filled practice as the following six steps:

The Process of Thought-Filled Practice

1. Select the role you have passion and strengths for doing.
2. Clarify the five critical aspects of that role.
3. Create simulations of the actual performance that allow you to focus on improving one or more of the role's critical aspects.
4. Gain relevant feedback from a skilled observer on the simulated performance in a timely manner.
5. Consider the feedback and make adjustments.
6. Repeat steps three to five for 10,000 hours.

Terry, what do you think about "thought-filled practice" and the role it plays in the off-season for the players?

Michler: I think sustaining thought-filled practice during the off-season is crucial to becoming a great soccer player. When the players are practicing after the high school season is over there are three simple steps for them to keep in mind: present, receive critique, and tweak.

They should present their skills in a practice or game, receive a critique from an experienced observer who hopefully is not too close to them like a parent or a friend, consider the advice, and tweak their performance as they feel it is appropriate.

Keep in mind that observation tells you what needs to be done. When my players are playing for a club team, they should conduct a game analysis, go back to practice to make refinements, and then go back to the game. The game will tell them if their desired objective has been achieved.

If not, then they need to go back to the drawing board and analyze the shortcomings. It's not practice that makes perfect. It's perfect practice that makes perfect. Do you know what it takes to make perfect practice? Repetition and repetition and then even more repetition are the answers. The response must become automatic.

Here is a great example from our CBC Dutch Touch camp last summer. Harry Jansen, a Dutch coach, was conducting a passing session with his group of players, which consisted of players from Holland and from the United States.

The drill was organized with four players to a group and one ball. The players were in a line across the field with about 30 yards from the deepest players. The sequence was player 1 passed to player 2 (about a seven-yard pass), player 2 returned the pass to player 1, player 1 then played a long pass (25 yards or so) to player 3, and then players 3 and 4 repeated the sequence and the ball returned to player 1.

There was nothing special per se about the drill. It was very basic. However, the attention to detail that Harry incorporated into each phase of the drill became VERY challenging to the players. Every part of the sequence had a SPECIFIC way that it needed to be done. He wanted the passes to be clean and precise, not casual and haphazard.

The quality of the passes, the position of the passes, and the direction and timing of the movements to get the ball back all had to be done in a CERTAIN way time and time again. Harry continued with this drill without any variation or break for 45 minutes!!!

He kept demanding that it had to be done the right way EVERY time. The players from the United States struggled with this because they are NOT used to this kind of technical discipline. They are used to just doing it without being critiqued and analyzed and forced to do it correctly every time.

Harry's message was about MASTERY of the technique and not just doing it for real purpose. He kept running the drill over and over. He made the players do the same thing endlessly until he was satisfied that it was getting better. It was a classic Dutch moment, and the Dutch players in camp were SO much better than our local players. They did it without any squawking while our players were getting restless and impatient.

My take on this was that our players have not been asked, or expected, to perform in that manner. We have a casual way of thinking that says just do it for the sake of doing it. The Dutch attitude was to do it right so it became an automatic process.

Management Insight

The best time to improve your performance as a manager is when you are not in the act of managing. Your "game time" is when you are managing. That's when you demonstrate your skills, but the improvement of your skills happens between the management moments.

You will steadily improve as a manager by identifying specific skills you want to improve, gaining feedback on your execution of those skills, tweaking aspects of those skills, practicing them over and over in the specific way you want to do them, and then trying them again in real management situations.

Maintain the Passion to Learn More and Always Innovate

Coughlin: How have you been able to improve your performance as the coach of the team while staying within the same organization for 39 years?

Michler: Every team is different. Every year presents new and different challenges. There is no place for complacency if I want us to be successful. It doesn't matter how many years I've been here. Each year is a unique situation that requires me to stay focused. If you're not changing or not current, then you're falling behind.

At the 2002 NSCAA Convention, a long-time college coach spoke and said something like, "I want to apologize to players I coached 25 years ago because I simply didn't know then what I know now." I feel that same way. A coach has to keep working to get better.

> *Management Insight*
>
> It doesn't matter how many years you've worked within your organization. What does matter is always looking for ways to be more effective in producing results.

Coughlin: Can you give me an example of how you've used the off-season to improve yourself as a coach.

Michler: The best example is when I got the opportunity from the NSCAA in 1997 to go to a 10-Day Coaching Symposium in the Netherlands. That changed everything for me. Since then my biggest influences have been coaches in Holland. I have worked hard to really understand the Dutch vision for soccer.

Too many times coaches make the game way too complicated. When I ask my Dutch friends, "What's new in the game? What's hot?" they always say, "Nothing is new. Just keep working to do it better, quicker, or smarter." Thank goodness for these guys. They are just so precise.

The Dutch teams are able to compete with much larger nations because of their teaching method. They compete successfully through education. They work to make the game simpler for the players. The biggest challenge is to always find a better way to make it simple. Too often what we do only complicates it. We need to fully realize the value and importance of simplicity. The Dutch say that the hardest thing to do is to simplify it.

When you put yourself out there you open yourself to what you don't know and your own insecurities. A lot of times people get a little bit of success and a little bit of knowledge, and they don't want anyone to mess with it.

Coughlin: What drove you to attend the 10-day coaching symposium in Holland in 1997 after you had already been the head coach for 25 years, won more than 600 games, and had three state championships? You were already the all-time winningest high school soccer coach in U.S. history by that point. What else did you have to prove?

Michler: It depends on what you're looking for. I've never coached because I wanted a certain number of wins. I wanted to learn more in 1997, and I still do. I wanted to get better. I wanted the opportunity to go to Holland to learn from some of the world's greatest soccer coaches.

It's about the learning and achieving the best performance possible. The keys are avoiding complacency, staying in the game, and trying to stay ahead of the competition. Once you think you're there, you are closer to being done than you ever realized. Nothing ever stands still. I'm a free thinker and I always want to improve my approach to coaching.

Management Insight

Are you working for a certain number or a certain honor or a certain salary? If that is what's driving you, you won't likely generate a great team performance.

The ultimate performer always wants to improve. The real test is what you do after you have all the highest honors. Are you still willing to push yourself to learn how to be a more effective manager?

Keep searching for ways to make your business simpler, not more complicated.

Perspective from Jan Pruijn, One of Terry Michler's Mentors

The 1997 Coaching Symposium had such a dramatic effect on Terry's growth as a coach that I decided to reach out to the person who taught the clinic. His name is Jan Pruijn. I called him in the Netherlands to gather his input on Terry Michler. At the time of the call, Jan was the Head of Technical for AJAX Cape Town and Director of Soccer Active. AJAX is one of the most successful professional soccer clubs in the world.

Jan holds a full coaching badge from the Royal Dutch Soccer Federation (KNVB), which allows him to coach at any professional level throughout the world. He was responsible for the establishment and organizational structure in the "AJAX-way" for branches in South Africa, Ghana, and Belgium.

He also worked with players and coaches in Japan at Urawa Reds, in China at CFA, Shanghai, in Spain at Real Sociedad, in Portugal at FC Porto, in Switzerland at FC Basel, and in England with several teams.

Here are Jan's thoughts on Terry Michler. I think what he has to say provides important implications for business managers.

Coughlin: What made Terry an effective student at your clinic?

Jan Pruijn: From the first moment on he showed his passion for learning by writing everything down. He had the discipline to write everything down and that increased the output of what he learned. He always took the lead in asking questions and leading the conversations.

Terry has a simple way of asking questions and sharing ideas. We had eight coaches together for 10 days for a clinic that was sponsored by the NSCAA. He was always organized and ready to engage in the learning process.

At the time I met Terry I did not know who he was or what his record was. He simply introduced himself to the group as "I'm Terry Michler from St. Louis, and I've been a high school coach for awhile."

Management Insight

Don't let your studies end in college. Throughout your career as a manager continue to take notes, ask questions, and engage people who know more than you in meaningful conversations. Don't get caught up in bragging about your accomplishments. Instead focus your energy on learning something new.

Coughlin: In your relationship with Terry through the CBC Dutch Touch program what has impressed you the most about him?

Pruijn: He wants to know everything in the game in the Dutch way. He still wants to study a lot of things that I give him from my end in order to improve as a coach. The biggest thing is if he has a challenge or something in his mind he gives it 100% until he brings it to a reality.

I brought up the Dutch Touch idea to him, and he ran with it. If he has a certain thing related to soccer or teaching youth, he goes. He looks at details. He is still a young dog in going after something and helping others.

Management Insight

Jan said this when Terry was 62 and heading into his 40th year as a coach. Do you still get excited about the details, and are you still open to learning how to improve?

Coughlin: What have you learned from Terry, and what affect has he had on your approach to teaching the game of soccer?

Pruijn: He showed me in certain ways that you have to be very patient to achieve what you're looking for. I have worked with the very best young players in Amsterdam. I have been a professional soccer player and coach in Holland since 1980. However, because of Terry I am more patient today and a bit more mature in coaching the players.

Management Insight

Jan had been a professional coach for almost 30 years at a very high level, and yet he was willing to learn from one of his students. What can you learn from your new employees?

Coughlin: Why do you think Terry has been such an effective coach for four decades?

Pruijn: One of the biggest things is Terry knows from his experience as a coach and from studying the game exactly the way to improve himself and his team and how to make that clear for his coaches and players. He combines his past coaching experience with the Dutch vision for soccer to improve the performance of his team.

Another key is that he doesn't jump from the Dutch vision to the French vision to the Brazilian vision to the German vision the way some coaches do. Some coaches constantly change their approach to coaching.

Terry knows what he expects, and he knows how to incorporate a single philosophy, the Dutch philosophy, which will always work in developing players. It may not guarantee championships, but it will always help in developing players in a consistent manner.

When he combines his own experiences as a player and coach with the Dutch philosophy, he develops what I call *The Terry's Way*. His approach is a simple and effective approach to soccer that doesn't change a lot every year.

Another major factor is that Terry is very humble and never makes coaching all about himself. With him there are four priorities: the soccer philosophy, the players, a lot of other things, and then him. He puts himself last. I've seen too many coaches where their names have to be on everything, and the team's achievements are all summarized under the coach's name.

Also, Terry is a good communicator who can be relied on to do what he says he will do. When he said he would stay in touch, he really did. He stays on top of the details of what he is promising to do.

Finally, Terry has great passion for the game. There are not that many people who love the game of soccer the way Terry does. He's made eight trips to Holland and every time he wants to find some insight that he can bring back to the United States and to his CBC soccer team. Time doesn't count when he's talking with someone about soccer.

Management Insight

Read back through those characteristics that Jan used to describe Terry. Are there any ideas in his comments that you think would be valuable for you to use at work? Which ones would you like to use and how can you put them into action in some small way immediately?

Coughlin: How do the Dutch soccer teams play with such an extraordinary degree of efficiency, and what is it that makes the Netherlands one of the highest-rated national soccer teams in the world?

Pruijn: There are Dutch-developed players who are on major teams in all of the major soccer countries.

By traveling all over the world conducting coaching clinics, I have seen some patterns as to why Dutch players and teams have been successful.

Holland is very small. Consequently we are able to put all of the best players in each age category in the same league. This way they are playing directly against the best competition on a regular basis. In the United States a great player in Boston might get to play against a great player in Los Angeles once a year if he is lucky. This same issue occurs in other very large countries.

Another advantage we have in Holland is we try to develop all the players in the same way. From the highest professional to the most amateur team, the training is similar throughout Holland. The consistency and quality of training is the same everywhere. We only have one governing soccer body in Holland. It's called the KNVB, which is the Royal Dutch Soccer Association.

In the United States there are all kinds of governing soccer bodies: the NCAA for college, all the different high school governing associations, and all the different club team associations. Every time a player moves from one team to another they have to learn a new approach to the game. In Holland that never happens. We have one soccer governing body, and one basic way of developing all of our players.

Also, the focus throughout Holland is on player development first and championships second. By keeping our attention on the development of players we are able to develop very technically sound soccer players. Consequently, during a game there are very few wasted passes or shots because the players' technical skills have reached such a high level.

Finally, every day in Holland we look in the mirror and ask ourselves, "What is happening with our team? What is working? What is not working?" Terry is very good at this as well. If you are not analyzing every day how to improve, then you will quickly fall backward. We are always looking to improve the performance of Dutch soccer.

Dutch soccer is about always looking back to improve the future. We are always looking for room for improvement. If you don't look backward, you can't improve in going forward.

Management Insight

Notice the importance of sticking with a given approach rather than changing it every couple of years.

What are the basic approaches to achieving results that you want your organization to sustain over the long term?

How can you increase the consistency and quality of employee development throughout your organization?

Coughlin: Terry, what is the difference between you as a coach in 2009 and you as a coach in 1994 and in 1979?

Michler: At each stage, I did what I thought I needed to do. However, you have to be able to adapt to the changes. In time you should mellow. 30 years ago I would really be upset if I didn't get through everything on my practice schedule. Today if I have four things scheduled to practice and I only get through three of them, I'm totally okay with that.

30 years ago I would lay out the practice schedule for the whole season in terms of when we would practice certain things. Today I would never do that. I adapt each practice to the needs of the team at each given moment.

Kids were much more independent 30 years ago. I could give them a ball and say "Go play," and they would create a game and start playing. Today if I did that the kids wouldn't know what to do. They want me to tell them to run a certain drill a certain way.

The people who do a lot of pickup games figure out how to do things on their own. In today's world kids are driven to an organized practice, and the coach runs them through drills. Their ball skills are better today, but they are not as independent of thinkers as they used to be.

30 years ago coaches got in a player's face. Today that totally doesn't work. You have to present yourself in a way that people can respond to. Sometimes you have to say things you normally wouldn't think to say in order to be effective with people.

Management Insight

To manage a group effectively, you need to understand the group, which includes understanding what approaches will and will not be effective with them at any given moment.

Focus on developing independent thinkers. If you run every minute of every meeting with your employees, you may end up with stronger technical employees who aren't as good at thinking independently as they can be.

Allow your employees the freedom to have conversations on their own where they can independently develop ideas to generate better results as a group.

Coughlin: Do you have any barrier-breaking goals for yourself that you focus on in the off-season?

Michler: One of my barrier-breaking goals is to know as much about soccer and to be as good at explaining it to my players as the Dutch coaches. 12 years ago I was this far away. (He holds his hands very far apart.) Now I'm maybe this far apart. (He moves his hands 50% closer.)

I've closed the gap considerably between what I know about soccer and what the coaches in Holland know. I may never get completely there, but that's what motivates me. It's an internal, subjective dream that I have, but it keeps me motivated.

Management Insight

You need to find a way to keep your passion alive in order to do the same for your group. What is some meaningful, barrier-breaking goal that you have for yourself?

Deal Directly with Difficult Times

Coughlin: In terms of winning state championships, your career has had three phases. In your first 18 years you won three state championships. Then you went 15 years without one. In the past six years you've won three more state championships. What were the 15 years in the middle like for you when you didn't win any state championships?

Michler: I started to question myself. I wondered to myself, "Have you just been lucky or what?" But in the end I didn't get too far away from what I believed in. I stayed with the general approach I always believed in, and I kept working to get better at it.

Management Insight

When times are tough and you are not achieving your desired results, stick with your basic values and beliefs. They will carry you through until better times arrive.

Refine Your Coaching Philosophy

Coughlin: In the Merriam-Webster Dictionary one definition of philosophy is "the most basic beliefs of an individual or group." Using that definition, what is your coaching philosophy?

Michler: It has been my good fortune over the years to have been influenced in soccer by some of the very best that the world has to offer. I have been mostly influenced by the Dutch style, as I have been a follower of Dutch soccer dating back to the days of "Clockwork Orange" and "Total Soccer."

Their free flowing style of play with precision passing and well-timed movements focused on going to goal is both exciting and challenging. It has been the basis of my coaching philosophy and is reflected in the playing style of my teams. In order to play that way you must train that way.

Training must reflect the demands of the game. The game determines what your training should be all about. The more game-like training becomes, the better prepared your team will be to play the games.

In my coaching experience, I have found that players learn best and respond more favorably to situations that they can identify as game-related. There always needs to be a connection between what you are doing in practice and how it will relate to what you need to do in the game. Making activities competitive builds enthusiasm because all players love to win.

The key to successful coaching is to be able to take players to a level that they could not get to on their own. That involves many things. You must create an environment where the players are comfortable and challenged. They must be enthusiastic and motivated. As a coach, you must be able to correct what needs to be corrected and know when to intercede and how to make things right.

A coach must have a very clear idea of what it is that he or she is trying to accomplish and what the end result should look like. If the technique is poor, do not let it continue without correcting it. I have a saying that I use: "you can get real good at being bad if someone does not step in and correct your faults." Repetition leads to habit, and if the repetition is done wrong, the outcome has no chance but to be wrong also.

A good coach must have an eye for detail. It is always the little things that matter the most. When coaches reach the higher levels of play, details become extremely important. Time on the ball is at a premium, and decision-making must always be done under pressure. If training is done under the watchful eye of a knowledgeable coach, then the players will benefit and the level of play will improve.

It has been my experience that in the biggest moments of the season when the game is on the line and a championship is in the balance the players who are best prepared for all that they will encounter will have the best chance for success. Training must be the means to the end. Train in the way that you want to play in the biggest games.

We had a team slogan in a championship season that was really simple: *Train and Trust!!* Trust that the training will pay off when you need it the most. Train in such a way that you can fall back on it in the time of greatest need or pressure.

One of the many experiences that I brought back from my soccer travels to Holland was the level of intensity in the training sessions. Both mental and physical intensity focused on hard and skillful play with a purpose was the standard and the expected norm. The outcome of the activity, exercise, or drill mattered. Nothing was casual or sloppy. Everything was crisp and clean.

There are really no deep, dark secrets for successful soccer. Tactics are wonderful, but if your technique is lacking, the tactics will have no chance.

Players must learn to be comfortable and accurate with the ball and develop the decision-making abilities to know what to do when and how to do it.

The application of technique in the right way at the right time is what allows tactics to be successful. The greatest tactical plan is dependent on the technical ability to execute the play successfully. Whenever you can combine technique and tactics into a training exercise, you are maximizing your time and enhancing the learning process.

I have nine areas that my basic beliefs regarding coaching fall under.

Terry Michler's Coaching Philosophy

1. *Teamwork*

    - Good teams combine good performance with good chemistry.
    - A good team is built upon the qualities of the players: technical, physical, and emotional.
    - Use proper training with emphasis on critical analysis and proper structure with high demands.
    - Technique and insight (tactical awareness) are the cornerstones for team success.
    - Formula for success: talent - effort - chemistry - coaching - luck.
    - Coaching: manage (organize), motivate, and evaluate – develop an action plan.
    - Coaches: informed, organized, structured, enthusiastic, passionate, and compassionate.

2. *Development*

- Develop the "soccer brain" in your players.
- Maintain a patient process over time: no short cuts.
- Mastery of technique (ball skills) is THE most important ingredient to success.
- Tactics and systems are very secondary to mastering technique.
- There is no system that makes up for poor technique.
- Quality touches: first and last touch, receive and release with accuracy and control.
- Technical development occurs in 3 stages: fundamental, game-related, and functional.
- Perfect practice makes perfect: repetitions of doing the right thing in the right way.
- Practice must resemble the game under pressures of time, space, and opponent(s).
- "Dry Swimming" training: you can't practice swimming on dry land, and you can't practice soccer without the elements of soccer: goals, opponents, rules, and direction.
- Tactical Training in three stages: individual, small group, and team.

3. *Technique – Touch*

- Keep-away versus give-away.
- Good, clean first touch allows more time on ball for next play (maintain possession).
- Bad first touch leads to turnover and fight back for ball or defend (loss of possession).
- Players must be able to use both feet equally well and all body parts comfortably.
- Receive, pass, move: the essence of attacking soccer.
- Two-touch play and mandatory two-touch passing develop passing and receiving skills.

- The higher the skill level is, the smaller the playing area becomes with more restrictions.
- The lower the skill level is, the larger the playing area becomes with fewer restrictions.

4. *Insight*

- An eye for the game: analytical.
- Take from the game to practice and back to the game.
- Small-sided games with various conditions: play to goals.
- Recognize and solve soccer problems as they arise.
- Know what to do while under pressure.
- Handle the complexity and unpredictability of the ever-changing situations.

5. *Tactics and Systems*

- Would you rather lose 2-1 or win 1-0? The difference could well be in breakdowns.
- Analysis of problems (breakdowns) and the correct solution(s) are critical.
- Develop plan based around team's strengths, not weaknesses.
- Identify team strengths and weaknesses.
- Devise a plan that will give the team its best chance to win.
- Tactics: options/choices – must always have at least two.
- Tactics: plan of action – team, small group, individual.
- System: alignment of player, back to midfield to forward, roles of each player/line.
- Style is about how you play: direct or possession or a combination of the two.
- Soccer's 3 Main Moments: we have ball, they have ball, and transition between the two.

6. *Team as an Orchestra*

    - Good individual qualities must all come together as one harmonious unit.
    - All the parts work for the good of the whole.
    - The coach acts a conductor by bringing all the parts together in cohesion.
    - The objective is to achieve a performance that is greater than the sum of its parts.

7. *Player Evaluation – TIPS (AJAX)*

    - **T**echnique: mastery of ball skills while under game pressure.
    - **I**nsight: a picture of everything that is going on around you with a solution in mind.
    - **P**ersonality: a winner's mentality, hate to lose, and a good team player.
    - **S**peed: physical, technical and tactical; speed of thought and play.

8. *Soccer is a Simple Game*

    - We complicate it. Walk before you run.
    - Master the basics and build from there.
    - Teach the game, know the game, and study the game.
    - In its simplest form, it is a game of opposites.
    - It comes down to many individual situations of 1v1.
    - Strive for numbers up whenever possible and take advantage.

9. *Fun*

    - The key is to have fun while working hard, learning, and improving.
    - Variety is the spice of life. Boredom kills enthusiasm.

- End each session with some sort of game or competition.
- Make the kids look forward to coming back for more.

My philosophy concludes with this thought: In soccer, the action of the legs is determined by the brain and the heart, or it is BUSY WITH BRAINLESS SOCCER.

Management Insight

What is your business management philosophy?

What are the basic beliefs that you want guiding your decisions and behaviors as a manager?

Keep a running list of your ideas and continue to refine it over time.

Give Back What You've Learned

Coughlin: You teach a free 8-week, 16-class course in the summertime on coaching soccer for coaches at all levels that anyone can attend. Why do you do that? You're giving away for free an incredible amount of information you've gathered over your career.

Michler: If I have something that is of value to other people, I'm happy to share it with them.

I always told myself when I was a young coach that if I ever got a chance to travel to other countries and learn about soccer that I would share everything I learned with anyone who wanted to listen.

Plus when I'm discussing the game with other coaches I always learn something. When I'm teaching Spanish at CBC I always tell my students, "I'm here today to see what I can learn from you."

On my first trip to Holland at our initial meeting with the group the instructor said, "There are two important points I want you to remember. First, I will go anywhere in the world to teach what I know about soccer. Second, when I teach I always have to learn something more." I've never forgotten that.

In the last several years people have taken me on as a resource partly because of my career and partly because of my website, which is www.cbcdutchtouch.com.

I try to give people advice that will increase their chances for success. I can't guarantee that they will win. On my website there are dozens of free diagrams on drills, articles, book reviews on soccer books, and a lot of other information. I try to provide people with advice that they can use with different age groups and different skill levels. I try to generalize as much as I can.

For little kids, you can't nitpick everything. It has to be fun. Just focus on a few broad concepts. I think the best youth coaches look at it as a process over time. They start it right, and they build it right. It's a process. They don't just recruit one superstar player, win a lot of games, and think they are done. They focus on helping players to improve over time.

Management Insight

When you teach, you will always learn something more. If you really want to strengthen your skill as a manager, be willing to share everything you've learned with anyone who wants to listen.

Perspective from Annie Beekman, One of Terry Michler's Proteges

Terry also spends a great deal of time in the off-season meeting with both experienced and new high school soccer coaches. He actively works to help them be more successful.

Annie Beekman has been the varsity head soccer coach for two years at Incarnate Word Academy High School. During that time she has won two Missouri Class 3 Girls High School Soccer State Championships. Terry Michler is one of her primary mentors.

In sitting down with Terry and Annie it became very clear to me why Terry is such an effective mentor for other coaches.

Coughlin: Annie, how long have you known Terry and in what ways have you gotten to know him?

Beekman: I first met Terry when I attended his soccer camp as a player 29 years ago. Then a year ago I met him again at the NSCAA Convention. He remembered me as "the blond girl who was always in motion."

I couldn't believe he remembered me. I asked if he would be willing to meet with me to answer some soccer questions I had. He said, "Sure. Give me a call. We can meet anytime." I didn't know if he was just saying that or if he really meant it.

When I did ask to meet with him, he set up a time right away and then really spent time with me. I couldn't believe it. He's my idol and I'm a brand-new head coach, but he sat down and gave me as much time as I wanted.

Management Insight

The great managers are willing to share. They don't care how long the other person has been in his or her role. If the other person is willing to learn, great managers are willing to teach and offer lessons they've learned through their experiences.

Are you willing to sit down with a new manager and share your insights?

Coughlin: Terry, what did you notice about Annie as you began to meet with her?

Michler: First, I could tell how much she wanted to learn. She was eager to learn and willing to really listen. Second, I knew she had self-confidence because she followed up with me and asked to sit down with me to go over some questions she had.

She also came as an observer to our camp last summer with a backpack and a notebook. She followed me all over at the camp and asked a ton of questions. This was after she had won two state championships in her first two seasons.

Management Insight

After you have had some significant early success are you still willing to ask questions and learn even more? An ongoing commitment to learning is crucial to continuous improvement.

Coughlin: Annie, what did you notice about Terry in your early meetings?

Beekman: His advice was so inspiring and simple. Every time I walked away from Terry I felt excited about coaching. He's a teacher, and he breaks things down when he explains an idea. He said several times, "Never get too far away from common sense. Keep it simple."

He explained his ideas both verbally and visually. He answered my question, but then he also showed me with a Power Point slide that he created while I was sitting there. Then he showed me variations of his point by moving the "players" around on the Power Point slide.

That alone was a great insight from him on how I can do a better job of teaching my players. He showed me how I can incorporate videos of our games with the Power Point slides and the verbal explanations. Another thing is I've watched him coach his own players, and he does a great job of adapting to different players and different learning styles. He is excellent at reading body language and sensing what a player needs at any given moment.

Michler: Annie's bringing up an important point about why great players don't necessarily make great coaches. Many times a great player succeeds because he or she has dominant athleticism or skills, but has never had to break the game down and explain it to someone else.

In England, great players get promoted directly into coaching positions and oftentimes fail. They were never prepared to be a coach. In Holland every Monday during the professional soccer season is set aside to teach current professional players how to be effective coaches.

When I was in Holland the first time I attended a coaching clinic on a Monday, and there were 20-30 professional players in attendance. They were being prepared to be coaches after their playing days were over. In Holland no one goes directly from the field as a player to the bench as a coach without preparation and education to coach.

Management Insight

Are you taking the time to teach your best salespeople and your best front-line employees how to effectively manage groups of people?

Many times I've seen star performers get promoted to management positions and fail miserably. They needed time, attention, and training to prepare to be a successful business manager before they were promoted.

Beekman: I also noticed right away how sincere and respectful Terry was when he explained things to me. He never talked about his record or his number of championships. He focused on helping me learn the game by simplifying it for me.

It's so exciting to talk soccer with Terry. I never feel like he's putting me down. I asked him how to use three forwards instead of two, which is what I always play with. He didn't act like I was stupid. Instead he showed me a variety of formations and then explained the roles and responsibility of each player in each formation.

He did it in a way that was very easy to understand. He broke the field down into a series of zones and explained what each player was supposed to do in her area. He drew a field like this on the chalkboard and showed me what should happen in each zone.

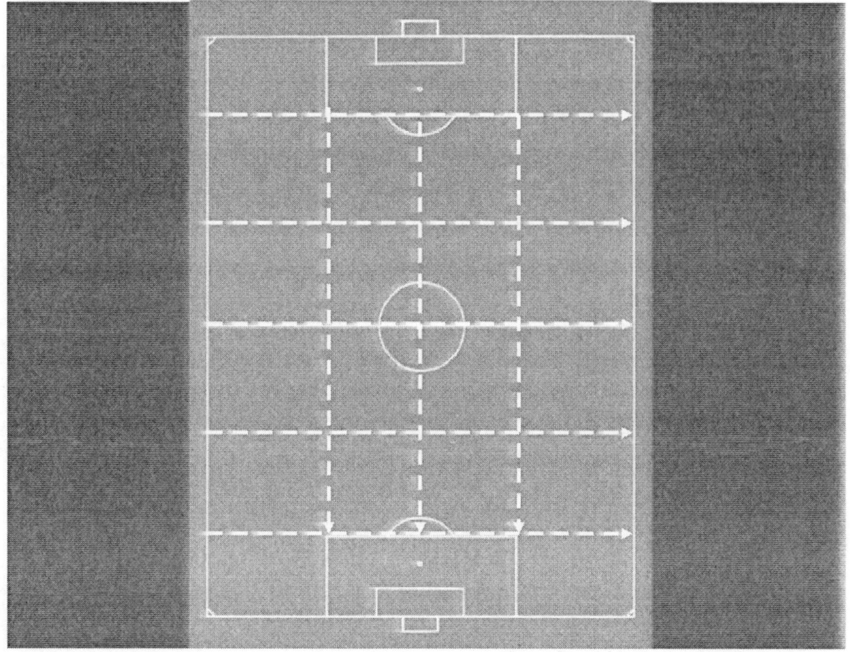

Management Insight

Great managers are teachers. They patiently explain to other people the details of what is important and why it is important. Always work to hone your skills as a teacher. Your impact as a manager will be much greater and last longer when you are the respectful teacher.

Beekman: Another really big thing Terry did for me was to keep reinforcing the importance of staying true to myself. I've been getting a lot of advice from a lot of people who want to pull me in a direction that is not the way I want to do things. Terry keeps encouraging me to stay the course in the basics and do things the way I believe in.

I would hear other people's ideas and think, "That just doesn't sound right." What Terry has done is to reassure me that my ways of thinking are effective.

Michler: A lot of people who give coaches advice are like a resort in a poor town. On my honeymoon we went to Acapulco. The resort was beautiful, but if we had veered off to the right or left we would have ended up in a really poor, dangerous area.

Many times people know one part of soccer, but if you ask them a question where they have to veer away from the one thing they know it becomes pretty clear that they don't have any real depth or breadth to their knowledge. Unfortunately, these are usually the people who constantly criticize coaches.

The biggest thing is I'm trying to convince Annie not to question herself. A lot of people will tell her she was lucky to have won those two state championships, that she inherited a ton of talent, and that's why she won. (He turns to Annie.)

Annie, you need to value what you've done. It didn't just happen because you had talent. You were the one who molded the talent into a championship team. Start by asking yourself what the end result was. Obviously it was great. Then ask yourself what you did to make it happen. Remember what you did. Don't let other people diminish what you did. No one can take that away from you. It's in the books.

Management Insight

The single best piece of career advice I've ever received was when I was just starting out at age 22. My college soccer coach, Dennis Grace, said, "Dan, just let Dan be Dan. Don't try to be someone you're not. If you try to act like a big shot, everyone is going to know it. Just be who you are and you will be fine."

There are a hundred ways to be effective as a manager, and there is one way that is guaranteed to fail. That one way is to be a chameleon. A chameleon is a lizard that changes its color to blend in with the surroundings.

Being a chameleon is good in the forest and bad in an organization.

A chameleon business manager is a person who changes his or her values and approach depending on who is in the room. Employees can't trust this type of manager, and he or she quickly loses credibility.

Just let you be you. Don't try to be someone you're not.

Coughlin: Have you found that Terry's ideas work in coaching girls? Is there anything he suggested that has not worked with girls?

Beekman: Everything he taught me works with girls. He said make appropriate demands of players, show caring and respect for every player, provide common courtesy to the players, and sincerely listen to their ideas. All of those things work with my players. The work rate and training sessions for the girls is very similar to the boys.

Perhaps one difference between girls and boys is that my players want a lot of one-on-one communication. They want to know why I'm doing what I'm doing. They feel more comfortable about things when I explain what is about to happen and why I'm doing it.

Actually, this is another thing I learned from Terry. On Sunday nights he e-mails a schedule to the players with what is going to happen each day for the next seven days. He explains what will be covered in each practice and where players need to be at certain times on each day.

I'm going to use that with my players this year. The more they know, the more relaxed they become. When they don't know what is happening is when we start to run into problems.

Management Insight

Too much has been made about managing men and women in different ways. The keys with all employees are to communicate with respect, caring, kindness, and sincerity.

Try to the best of your ability to let your employees know what is coming up and why it will be happening. This is another way of demonstrating respect for them.

Coughlin: What have you learned from Terry about player selection?

Beekman: I always knew that the foundation of a great player is having great touch with the ball and great speed. Terry has really emphasized over and over for me intangibles such as mental toughness, the ability to ignite the team in a positive way, being a good school citizen, and representing the school well.

He's also taught me that it's okay to take a chance on a player who may be struggling because something is bothering her. With a player like that, I've learned the importance of spending one-on-one time and just listening to her. Sometimes that's all she needs to calm down and start to really play well.

Michler: Another idea on player selection that I learned from Bob Shannon, our former football coach, is, "Look for players you can lose with." I want players who care about winning and who give 100% effort toward trying to win every game. Then if we lose, I can live with that. It's the players who don't really care about winning that can really wear me out.

Beekman: Ok, add that to my list of things I've learned from Terry. I really like that idea of selecting players I can lose with.

Management Insight

What are your beliefs about employee selection? What do you look for in the employees you hire for your organization? Create interview questions, case studies, and role plays that will help you find the employees you want.

Coughlin: Annie, do you have any other thoughts about Terry and what makes him effective as a coach?

Beekman: He has an incredible passion for soccer and for learning how to be a better coach. It's obvious that he loves what he does. I'm like that. I love coaching. I didn't coach at all for five years when I was raising my daughters, and I really missed it.

I'm never going to make a lot of money doing it. I just want to give the players a great experience both on and off the field when they are on my team. I want to keep improving all the time. Terry inspires me because he's still just like that.

Michler: I'm just like Annie when I'm with the Dutch coaches. I'm like a kid in a candy store. My Dutch friends make the game simple. A lot of coaches want the gimmicks. They look at my stuff, and they say, "That's it. That's too simple. Where's the good stuff?" I say, "It is simple, and that's why it is the good stuff."

> *Management Insight*
>
> As I watched Terry and Annie interact for 90 minutes a new phrase popped into my mind: overlapping passions. When you are searching for an effective mentor, look for someone whose passions overlap with yours.

Select Captains

Coughlin: How are the captains of the team selected?

Michler: Captains can make or break a team. I have let the team pick them and I have picked them. As I got older (and wiser) I picked them. The key to a good captain is that the rest will follow him. All the championship teams had strong leaders.

> *Management Insight*
>
> Carefully select the people you put in charge of important projects. Is the person a strong leader, will the members of the team respond effectively to his or her leadership, and can the person guide the group to the desired outcome in a sustainable way?

Chapter Four

Preseason

The preseason lays the foundation for all that is to come.

In business, the "preseason" is the time when a manager prepares his or her group for a new project, initiative, or client. In soccer and in business, this is the time for selecting members of the team, clarifying expected behaviors, establishing championship habits, and setting barrier-breaking objectives.

Define a Team

Coughlin: How do you define a team and what does it take to build a great team?

Michler: A team is a group with a common focus that works together to achieve a common goal.

First, you need basic talent. I take the best players available regardless of what year in school they are in. On the very first team back in 1970 I had a freshman starting on the varsity. So I evaluate the available talent and I select the very best players regardless of how old they are. You need all the right ingredients to build a championship team.

Then you need to get players to buy into a common purpose. At CBC tradition plays a big part in getting the players to focus. They are part of a soccer program that has been very successful for over sixty years.

Management Insight

Does your group have a common focus? Are all the members working together to achieve a common goal? Does your group have the basic ingredients necessary for success? Are you selecting the very best talent for your organization regardless of the person's age? These are the starting points to eventually achieve extraordinary results as a group.

One thing I give to the players is my description of what a good team looks like. Here it is:

Terry Michler's Characteristics of a good TEAM

TEAM -- Together Everyone Achieves More

1. Work together for common goals.

    - Prepare well in practice and pre-game.
    - Take what you do seriously.
    - Constantly work to become better.
    - Be open for advice and constructive criticism.
    - Work and play to the best of your ability in the best interest of the team.
    - Put TEAM interests ahead of personal interests.
    - Good players don't automatically make good teams.
    - Be positive when dealing with teammates.
    - Communicate to teammates in ways that are helpful and meaningful.

2. Make the game easier for the team and yourself.

    - Play quick, simple, and effective soccer.
    - Work hard, play smart, and be productive.
    - Play within the concept of the game plan.
    - Do not allow opponents any opportunity to play.
    - Don't repeat the same mistakes.
    - Don't let mistakes get you down.
    - Tell teammates "man on" or "turn."
    - Concentrate on your tasks throughout the game.
    - Position yourself in the right place at the right time.
    - Do the right thing in the right way (touch).
    - Anticipate the possibilities that might develop.

3. No regrets.

    - No "If I would have done this." Leave it ALL on the field.
    - Play to win each half of the game.
    - Play from the first whistle like you do at the last whistle when the game is on the line.
    - Discourage teams very early on by finishing chances within the first 5 -10 minutes of the game.
    - Make your commitment equal to your ability. Be determined to play your best game possible.
    - Out-work, out-think, and out-play the opponent for the entire game.
    - Play every minute of every game as if it were the most important game.

Select Players

Coughlin: If you have to choose between a superior soccer player with a bad attitude and a poor work ethic, and a person with a great attitude and great work ethic but below average soccer skills and mediocre physical traits, what do you do?

Michler: You want to try to work the first case until you see no hope. Many times a good give-and-take conversation reveals reasons for the bad attitude, and then you can work through those reasons.

You would never just want to dismiss that player without exhausting all the avenues first. Many times players use those negative behaviors as defense mechanisms to cover up low self-esteem and insecurities. Sometimes when you give those people more and more responsibility, they really take off.

Of course, this is not always the case. There are times when you are dealing with a real jerk who wants NO PART of what you're offering. If you keep him, he can ruin the team. By cutting him it is addition by subtraction. In the end these types of people will more often let you down than fulfill any promise of potential.

The other type you asked about will never reach great heights of performance as soccer players, but given a certain role on the team they can and do become very useful and helpful. You could not build a successful team with a team of just those types, but they can be a part of a successful team.

Building a team to me is like putting a puzzle together. No two pieces are ever really the same, but they still have to fit together to complete the puzzle. Every piece has its place where it fits comfortably. The key is to identify the individual qualities of the players and then weave them together into a cohesive unit where each person is doing his thing in the best interest of the team as a whole.

Management Insight

Managers sometimes fool themselves into believing that a person with a great attitude and work rate can suddenly become technically very proficient and significantly improve business results. Then the manager becomes very frustrated and upset when the individual doesn't contribute in an extraordinary way.

Technical skills and knowledge are very important. They need to be sought out in the recruitment process. The individual without technical strength may help the group, but an organization with only these types of performers will not achieve greatness.

I was impressed by Terry's honesty about the second type of player. These types of individuals "will never reach great heights of performance as soccer players."

Then notice how Terry is willing to invest time with a high potential performer who has a bad attitude. He's explaining the upside of uncovering insecurities and helping a person move past a lack of self-esteem.

Clarify Values and Expected Behaviors

Coughlin: What type of rules or expected behaviors do you put in place during the preseason?

Michler: I don't set tight itemized rules. I want the players to be responsible for their own behavior. If that happens, I give them leeway. I want them to think for themselves. They're in charge of their behavior. If we run into problems, then there are consequences. I do hand out my expectations for them during our preseason. Here is what they receive:

CBC Soccer: Expected Behaviors

1. Respect and uphold the strong CBC Soccer Tradition. Meet the challenge to be the best and be proud of your efforts.

2. Be ready to give your best effort (physical, mental, technical, and tactical). Work hard for the first goal, shutout, and to win both halves.

3. Don't settle for second best. Challenge yourself and your teammates to be the best.

4. Strive to achieve established team goals. Establish a purpose and make that be your focus.

5. Work hard, listen, cooperate, and get along with teammates and coaches. Team unity (chemistry) is a vital ingredient to success.

6. Respect your teammates. Be positive, supportive, and together. Avoid negative criticisms and put downs.

7. Know your role on the team and do your best to fulfill it.

8. Be on time for meetings, practices, and games. Any absence or tardiness must be personally cleared through the coach by the player himself.

9. Be a good school citizen. Maintain good grades and stay out of disciplinary troubles (tardiness, detentions).

10. Have proper clothing and equipment for all types of conditions (weather and surface).

11. Be responsible for all uniform items. Keep them clean and in good condition. Report any problems immediately. Any lost or damaged items may become your responsibility.

12. Game day: shoes shined, uniform clean and worn properly, shirt in, socks up, no long undershorts, and nothing that will detract from the uniform (when we wear white, nothing colored underneath.)

13. Use of alcohol, drugs, and tobacco will NOT be tolerated. Any violation will be dealt with and could result in your dismissal from the team!!! All violations will be evaluated on an individual basis!!!

14. Report all injuries and illness immediately to your coach. Follow up with treatment/rehabilitation as prescribed. No one will be expected to play hurt or sick.

15. Realize that game performance is largely determined by your practice work ethic. Habits are formed and evaluations are made by what you do in practice.

16. CBC Soccer is a competitive situation. In order to be competitive, improvement and development must be ongoing. This means both in-season and especially during the off-season. Don't cheat yourself. Be prepared, work hard, and train properly. Remember this: when you're not practicing and someone else is, when he meets you, he may well beat you. Be ready!!!

Michler: In addition to those expectations on behavior, I give the players a set of expectations on their attitude. Here is what it looks like:

CBC Soccer: Expected Attitudes

1. A big win against a big team can easily be followed up by a big letdown. Don't be an easy target for an upset. Stay focused all of the time and RESPECT EVERY OPPONENT! Remember that when a lesser team beats a better team, especially a high-profile top-ranked team, it literally makes their season.

2. Be aware that the CBC Game is the BIG GAME for most of our opponents. Even though you may not feel the game to be really important, it is THE game for most of our opponents. Be ready. Don't let down.

3. Accept constructive criticisms from coaches in a positive way. Don't act like you are being picked on!! Comments made from coaches to players are meant to be helpful, insightful, or motivational. The real time to worry is when the coach says nothing.

4. Help out with the little things. Don't expect someone else to do it. Equipment is provided for the players' benefit. Be available and take an interest in helping when help is needed. Don't take things for granted.

5. Respect your teammates. Team chemistry is vital to our success. Do your best and encourage the rest to do theirs. Speak by example. Team unity is the invisible thread that makes a big difference in all successful teams.

6. Don't allow a mistake, failure, or an opponent to cause you to break down and lose your cool. Maintain self-control at all times.

7. Smile on the outside and burn on the inside. Turn frustration into motivation and regain the edge. Don't lose concentration!!

8. Don't taunt or intimidate. Work hard, play smart, and be productive.

9. Throughout the course of the game, there will be plenty of time to rebound and regain. Don't panic.

10. Believe in yourself and your teammates. Be positive and keep faith. There is strength in numbers. Be together!!

Management Insight

Keep expectations clear and simple, not vague and complicated. After a person reads them he or she should know very clearly what to do and what not to do without having every possible situation spelled out.

Reinforce Championship Habits

Coughlin: How do you use the preseason to reinforce habits that can be sustained all the way to the state championship?

Michler: The preseason sets the tone for the year. We start with the reality that all of the players have been away from us for at least eight months. During that time they have all played club ball and have had to adapt to new and different demands.

Our starting point is ground zero, and we begin to build from there. We realize from the very beginning that this is a process that extends throughout the entire season. It only starts during the preseason, but a good start usually goes a long way.

From the very beginning when we take roll for the first day and have the very first contact with the players, we are "in the zone" of what the year will be all about. We welcome them and from the first moments we begin to imprint them with the CBC Soccer Mentality, our expectations, and our goals for the year.

We will not allow the standard to slip. Our demands are high and we let them know we mean business from the get-go. When a drill or exercise is not going right, we stop it, correct it, and resume. We continue to stop the drill as necessary until we are satisfied with how it is being done.

For most of the players, this is the first "reality check" for them. They may be able to get away with careless and sloppy play elsewhere, but not here. Once that resonates with them then the standard has been set and they know the expectation. Day after day that demand is always in place.

The same holds true for off-the-field situations. We demand a high performance on and off the field. Players must accept responsibility for their actions by being on time, in the right training clothes, and fully focused.

We regularly check on their classroom progress as well and will sit players down if their grades are unacceptable. Consistency is the key, and fortunately for us the coaching staff is very much in tune with that concept. The players realize early on that there are no ways around it. The tradition of our program demands the very best and that starts from day one and continues every day until we finish the season.

Management Insight

New employee orientation meetings are important. They help a new employee understand what is expected of him or her and where to turn for assistance.

However, don't stop there. At least once a year provide orientation for all of your employees on what is expected from them and what they can expect from you. Reemphasize what is important in your organization.

Build a Tradition Based on Excellence

Coughlin: How do you talk about the tradition of CBC Soccer during the preseason? How do you focus on tradition with your players during the season and during the state tournament?

Michler: Tradition motivates a CBC Soccer player. The tradition of CBC Soccer is a rich, lengthy, and successful one. The average season record for a CBC Soccer team is 20 wins, 5 losses, and 3 ties, and that is against the best competition and against teams dying to beat us. That record for many teams would be a special season. It would be considered a great season. For CBC it's like getting a "C" in the classroom.

We emphasize the CBC Soccer Tradition with stars above our soccer logo. Each star represents a state championship and every CBC player strives to add another star. Next year every item of CBC clothing from game jersey to T-shirts will have the same seven-star logo on it.

We define tradition as what the past has accomplished and has thus established as a platform for the present, and what the present can do to continue to challenge the future teams. The tradition concept is like a chain link with the past connected to the present and the present to the future. We want our players to leave a legacy for the future players to aspire to and be motivated to improve on.

Many of our former players may be fathers, brothers, or uncles of the current players. During the year former players will stop by and talk to the players or send emails to encourage or congratulate the players. CBC Soccer remains an important part of the lives of many people as it continues to be a source of pride and success.

Management Insight

Regardless of how long you have been with your current work team or how long your organization has been in business, you can talk about the importance of tradition.

You're either carrying on the great tradition from the past or working to establish a great tradition for the future. In either case you're helping your employees to lift up above the day-to-day activities and focus on leaving a great legacy behind.

Set Barrier-Breaking Objectives

Coughlin: What types of goals do you set for the team during the preseason?

Michler: I learned from an English coach about goal setting. He said there are three different types of goals: a security goal, a realistic goal, and a barrier-breaking goal.

A security goal is achieving what you know you can do. A realistic goal is one you know you can achieve if you play at your best, but you have to be at your best to achieve it. A barrier-breaking goal is one you may never achieve, but you want to pursue it anyway.

If you only have security goals, then that saps your energy. You don't have anything to get your competitive juices flowing. As long as you always have a barrier-breaking goal, it keeps the passion going. We have four types of objectives for each season: themes, result goals, barrier-breaking goals, and process goals.

For example, for my 2004 team the objectives we handed out during the preseason were as follows:

Themes:

LAST TEAM STANDING (Celebrate with the trophy after the state final.)

TRAIN AND TRUST (Train honestly every day, and when the pressure is the greatest rely on training to get through the tough times.)

Result Goals:

1. Beat our top two rivals.
2. Win all tournaments.
3. Win one game at a time.

Barrier-Breaking Goals:

1. Win every game.
2. Win the last game of the year.
3. Break the record for most wins in a season. (32 wins are the most by any CBC team that I have coached.)

Process Goals:

1. Prepare to win, improve every day, and perform to win.
2. Expect to win. Be confident, but not cocky or arrogant.
3. Develop a winner's mentality. Win with style and dignity.
4. Be together as a team. Accept your role on the team.
5. Stay focused. Avoid distractions (rankings, message boards.)
6. Work hard, play smart, be productive, and give us a chance to win.
7. Find a way to win. First Goal + Shutout = Win
8. Battle through adversity. Tough times don't last, tough people do.
9. Be responsible for yourself at all times. Act appropriately.
10. Be a TEAM – Together Everyone Achieves More.

Chapter Five

Regular Season

One of the greatest management challenges is to convert routine day-to-day activities into opportunities for constant growth and improved results.

During September and October the CBC Soccer Team plays 16 regular season games. In addition the team plays three regular season tournaments, which I will discuss in the next chapter.

These eight weeks are analogous to a manager's regular flow of work throughout the entire year. The virtual nonstop flow of games and practices is similar to the on-going meetings, phone calls, employee situations, crises, and projects that managers face every day.

By digging into the details of the regular season for a high school soccer team, my hope is you will find some practical insights that you can use on an everyday basis to elevate your impact as a business manager.

Provide Leadership

Coughlin: Terry, I define leadership as "influencing how other people think in ways that generate better sustainable results both for the organization and the people in it." How do you provide leadership as the head coach?

Michler: As a leader, I try to develop problem-solvers. I want to put the other person in a position to think. It's about the thought process. When you are in a game like soccer that is so fast-paced and constantly changing you have to think for yourself. In our training sessions we put the players into game-like situations where they have to think. In the games we expect our players to solve the problems on their own.

For example, in the 2009 state quarterfinal game we went down by a goal with ten minutes left. One of our captains, Austin Tierney, took charge. We had put players in that situation many times in practice so he had already thought through what he needed to do.

A leader gets people to do more for themselves rather than hovering over them and solving all their problems. You have to let them rise and fall on their own. Don't hover over them. Kids today are hovered over too much.

When a player asks me what to do in a certain situation, I usually respond with another question. I used to feel pressure to always provide the player with an answer, but as time has gone by I've learned to ask the player questions and get him to think for himself.

I'll ask the player, "What do you think you should do in that situation?" I want him to develop his soccer brain. I will provide the player with a framework to work from, but I want him to make his own decisions.

> *Management Insight*
>
> The job of a leader is to develop problem-solvers and people who can think for themselves. Enough said.

Establish a Style of Performing

Coughlin: In your book, *Total Dutch Football*, you talk about the importance of playing with a certain style that emphasizes a precise, creative, and attacking approach to every game. This is a style you really learned in great detail from the Dutch coaches. Why is this style so important?

Michler: Confidence and control!!! When you can play in such a way that the other team struggles to keep up, you have a distinct advantage. Soccer is a game determined by your ability to use the ball. Ball possession and attacking with ball possession give you that advantage. Some teams practice possession soccer, but they don't play attacking ball possession soccer.

In soccer, ball possession is NEVER an end product. It is the MEANS to the end. As the Dutch would say, the key is ball possession in order to build a controlled attack that leads to goals. Our focus is not merely on ball possession for the sake of ball possession. That does NOT lead to goals.

The confidence factor was evident in the state finals as our team played in a way that looked like they were having fun in a championship game before 5,000 people against a team that had beaten us twice previously during the season. Our players were "on their game" and it showed. They were enjoying the moment.

The training in the week leading up to the final game was intended to produce that effect. We emphasized quick, clean ball possession with the end result always going to goal. The players were well rehearsed in how they were to play, and they played a near perfect game.

Creative individualism within a team framework is the ultimate challenge to conquer. We did it as the final game showed. We had players who were dominating in their individual roles, both in the attack and in defense, but it was also demonstrated in the performance of the team.

The team framework must include the individual qualities of the players. The better players have a responsibility to do more. That's their role; nothing more, nothing less, and with no unnecessary fanfare. As you put together your playing concept, it must be a combination of both team and individual and blended in the best way possible to create a maximum performance.

Management Insight

An attacking, ball possession style is exactly what the best businesses in the world use. They keep possession of the ball by taking great care of their customers. That keeps them in the game, but they don't settle for just keeping their current customers by doing really well what they've always done.

They also probe for ways to create and deliver more value to their customers and their potential customers. This attacking mentality is how these managers expand their lead.

They challenge themselves to come up with innovations that add more value to their desired customers and move their results forward in a sustainable and profitable way.

Great managers foster creative individualism within the framework of the organization. They empower their employees to make decisions on their own within the framework of the organization's values and purpose.

These great managers want creative, daring employees who are willing to take on the responsibility of creating and delivering continually greater value to customers and prospects.

Perspective from Sean Kuster, One of the Captains on Terry Michler's 2009 State Championship Team

Sean Kuster was a four-year member of the CBC Varsity team. As a senior he was First Team All-State and First Team All-Midwest. I asked for his thoughts on playing for Terry Michler.

Sean Kuster: Mr. Michler's ideas on what makes for an effective playing style allowed me to excel with my playing style. In practice we spent a lot of time working on combination games and penetrating the defense. We didn't just possess the ball. We learned to attack forward with speed and confidence while keeping the ball within the team and not just kicking long balls.

We had great discussions about what we needed to do to warm up and improve our skill. He helped us get in the game mentally and be physically prepared for every game, but he also told us that when it came down to game time it was all about us wanting to play and having the passion to win games.

The main thing I learned from Mr. Michler about soccer is that high energy on and off the ball is the key to success. I learned that the first and last touch on the ball affects how you play a lot. I also learned to understand the game from a coaching point of view. He taught me to take the game seriously and always focus before and after the game.

Beyond soccer, I learned from Mr. Michler about being a leader. He taught me to take the right approach in always being ready for whatever comes at you, good or bad, easy or hard. I learned to always give everything I have at 100%. His one-on-one talks with me on things I needed to work on to improve really helped me. I always felt inspired.

Some of my favorite sayings from him are "train everyday as if it were a game day," "eat right before and after a game," "hydrate a lot," "perfect practice makes perfect," and "improve always."

He has been coaching for a long time and knows the schools we play against very well. He knows the system they each play and their strategies. It is a gift that he can recognize these things. He will know the formation, their setup, most of their key players, and the system they play.

He explained to us the best way to defend and attack each team, but he also said that it was up to us to do that in any way, shape, or form. He told us that the words and formations were just guidelines to help us succeed.

During the state tournament, he knows that it all comes down to one game and one game only. We took one game at a time. We focused on one game and nothing else. We were not going into the games cocky, but confident that we would play well.

We never questioned each other. We had faith and trust in each other. He knew I played different from other people. As long as I could make my style work and work within the team concept, he didn't question me.

He gave us hints and advice, but he told us that at this age we should be capable to play the game freely on our own. He is a great coach and no one could have a better one to help lead them to victory.

Clarify Each Role

Coughlin: How do you determine the best role for each member of the team?

Michler: First, develop a role for each player. As I mentioned the better players have bigger roles with more responsibilities, but they are still just doing their role. Everyone on our team has a role. I make it very clear what each player is supposed to do in that role. Every player is expected to fulfill his role as well as he can.

I'm big on "paired opposites." One year I had a lightning fast forward so I paired him with a really skillful player. If there was a long pass into an open space, the fast player's role was to run onto the ball. If it was a shorter pass on the ground, it was the more skillful player's role to gather the ball in and distribute it.

Throughout the entire team we find paired opposites so that players can complement one another in what they are doing. Everybody has a vested interest this way, and they're all part of the outcome. This way everyone is much more motivated to do a great job because our team depends on each player successfully fulfilling his role.

Management Insight

In your organization, does every member of the group understand the responsibilities of his or her role?

Is each individual paired with someone who brings complementary strengths?

Do the members of your group have a vested personal interest in the success of the team? Do they feel that the team might fail if they don't fulfill their individual roles?

Focus on talent management, which includes organizing individual talent into "paired opposites" that can make each part of the organization stronger.

Integrate Superstars

Coughlin: How do you get extremely talented soccer players who are the stars on great club teams to pull together and support one another on your team?

Michler: I don't value a star concept. I don't make a big deal about postseason awards. After we won the state championship this year, we had a couple of players who were named All-American and one player who was named Player-of-the-Year in St. Louis, but I don't make a big deal about that.

I don't want the players who did their roles as well as they could and were very successful in doing so to feel bad because they didn't get the big honors.

I don't want a star system because if everything depends on the star player and he has a bad day, then we lose. This year we had different players step up every game. The other teams couldn't just concentrate on stopping one player.

One way we foster teamwork is to have every CBC soccer player at all levels from varsity to the freshmen team wear the exact same practice uniforms. On Mondays they all wear certain colors. Then on Tuesday they have different colored practice uniforms, but they are the same at all levels.

The players pay for the practice uniforms at the beginning of the season, and then they get to keep them. I brought that idea back from the European club teams. It helps build a sense of pride in being a part of the team, and it also helps to break down the star system. It doesn't matter if a player is All-American or the third string player on the freshmen team. He still wears the same practice uniform as everyone else for that day.

Management Insight

Teamwork is not complicated to explain, but it's not easy to build either. Avoid the star system that makes it seem that one or two star performers generated all of the results.

Just as better soccer players get more playing time and bigger college scholarships, certain employees will get better projects and bigger salaries.

However, all employees can be treated with an equal degree of respect.

Score the First Goal

Coughlin: You've talked about the importance of scoring the first goal in a game. Why is that so important to the team's success?

Michler: The first goal changes the dynamics of the game. It relaxes one team and stresses the other, and then the mental toughness of the teams becomes a bigger factor in who will win.

If our team has the lead and is mentally tougher than our opponent, we will win most of the time. At CBC from 1979 to 2009, when we scored the first goal in the game our record is 600 – 21 – 30.

Over time there became a belief that if we score first we will win. We believe we should win if we score first, and chances are we will win. Soccer is a game that averages low scores. 1 – 0 is a common score in soccer. Scoring that first goal will win every game that ends 1 – 0!!

Additionally, there is a psychological edge achieved when we score first. When you combine a history of success with that edge a huge momentum shift occurs by scoring first. The first goal relieves pressure, improves confidence, and provides a more relaxed state of mind.

Management Insight

If your organization can get to the marketplace before anyone else with a new product or service that is of real value for customers, the chances are much better that you will win a greater share of the revenue and profits than your competition.

If you do that successfully over a number of years, the people in your organization will start to believe that every time they get to the marketplace first with great value they will win significantly more revenue and profits than anyone else.

This will increase everyone's sense of urgency in your organization to "score" first before the competition can get into the market with a certain type of product or service.

Observe for Detailed Understanding

Coughlin: You talk a lot about the importance of observation. Why is observation so important in terms of generating a great team performance?

Michler: To me observation is what separates the different levels of expertise. Some people see some things, and other people see everything. Some people can see things almost before they happen!

I once attended a coaching clinic, and the presenter was a U.S. coach of the highest order. He was a professional coach in our professional league, and he started the session by talking about a painting.

He said that most people could acknowledge the painting for what it was and what it presented, but a very few when looking at it from a slightly different approach would see "a cat in the picture." They were able to see more in the picture because of their ability to observe in a different and more detailed manner.

When people watch a game they all see it in their own way. Most see it like the plot in a novel and simply retell what happened, but the gifted observer will see the same game in a different way, much like knowing the theme in a novel as opposed to the plot.

When I attended the Coaching Symposium in Holland in 1997 we learned that one of the biggest precepts of Dutch Soccer is Game Analysis. The very first day we went to a professional game and were paired with another member of our group. Each pair was given a specific assignment to observe and report on the following day. The assignments were quite limited, but they progressively increased with each game that we observed.

I was overwhelmed by the detail that went into the observation of our instructors. As we saw the plot they saw the theme. As we continued watching more games, we gradually drifted away from the plot and started closing in on the theme. When I observe a soccer game today I "see the cat" and am all about the theme.

A soccer game unfolds differently to the casual observer than it does to the trained observer. It's all about what you are looking at and looking for. It's the perspective that you take, and then it becomes how you apply it.

Observe, embrace, and apply. In the preparation for the state championship game in 2009, I had the chance to observe our opponent a few weeks earlier in their district final game.

Having played them twice I knew enough about them already, but I wanted to fine-tune my final observation. I only focused on them in a game that was evenly contested and decided by one goal. Had they lost that game my day would have been totally wasted, but that was not to be.

I applied the information from that observation in a game plan for the state championship hoping against hope that we would be in that game and that they would be our opponent. As luck would have it that's exactly how it turned out. Our game plan turned out to be good, and the execution of it by our players was perfect.

Management Insight

Spend far more of your time observing your employees in action than telling them what to do. Individuals will be much more open to hearing what you have to say if they know your comments are based on careful observation.

Observe your customers as well. Always search for a better understanding of what your customers want and/or need. Your observations can help to improve the current delivery of value and increase the chances of coming up with a new product or service that will really be a breakthrough value for your customers and prospects.

Finally, carefully observe your competition. They may have an area of strength or weakness that you can quickly convert to your organization's advantage.

Evaluate to Improve Performance

Coughlin: How do you evaluate your team's performance?

Michler: I do it a few ways both for the team as a whole and for each player that gets into the game. For every game we have 10 measures of success.

CBC Soccer Game: Measures of Success

1. Play as though we're down by three goals at the start of the game.
2. Score the first goal.
3. Score the second goal in the next ten minutes.
4. Get a shutout.
5. Win both halves.
6. Play as though it were the state final game.
7. Defend, build up the attack creatively, and finish.
8. Keep the opponent to less than 10 shots.
9. Score two second half goals.
10. Overcome the 0-3 start by outscoring the opponent by more than three goals.

After the game, I let them know how they did on each of those ten measures. I also post my positive comments on the game and my areas of concern. Then I rate the team's performance for each game on a scale from 10 to 1 where:

10 is brilliant
9 is outstanding
8 is excellent
7 is solid
6 is adequate
5 is fair
4 is below average
3 is poor
2 is lousy
1 is embarrassing

Over the course of the season I connect the dots for each game rating so the players can see the trends we are on as a team. I can also look back at any team I've coached and see the trends that happened during their particular season. All of this helps me to improve my insight and my understanding of what needs to be done.

On an individual basis I give each player that got into the game a rating on the same 10 to 1 scale and a comment.

Also, before the season I have each player take a psychological profile test. The results of that test help me to understand each player's individual needs. I go over the results with each player to help him better understand himself.

From two books, *Focused on Soccer* by Bill Beswick and *On Soccer* by Sven-Goren Eriksson, I assembled 13 questions to ask each of my players. The player's answers provide me with a psychological profile. Here are two of the questions. Some are much longer.

Sample Question #1: Place a check in front of the line that best describes you: _ "I must, I should, I've got to." _ "I want to, I'll have a go, I can."

Sample Question #2: Circle any and all of the words that create pressure for you as a soccer player:

Family
Coaches
Referees
Media
Fans
Teammates
Medical
School
Team in a Slump
Change of Coach
Change of Position
Loss of form
Injury
Mistakes
Personal Problems
Family Problems
Media Attention
Lifestyle Problems
Nonselection
Change of Tactics

Management Insight

Are you investing the right amount of time in evaluating what has just happened and letting the members of the group know your thoughts on their performance both collectively and individually?

Are you being honest in your evaluations about what really happened or are you giving evaluations based on what other people said about their performance?

CBC plays over 30 varsity soccer games every year with 15 to 25 players getting into each game. Notice the incredible commitment Terry makes to evaluate the group's performance as a whole and the performance of each individual within the group.

When I looked at his ratings for all the games in one season I noticed that over half of them were "adequate" or lower on his scale. The team that year won over 80% of its games. I was impressed by the honesty of Terry's evaluations. Just because his team won a very high percentage of the games didn't mean he rated all those games as outstanding or brilliant.

Increase Purposeful Efficiency

Coughlin: You said "the game is all about using the ball in the most efficient way." I've never heard that before. What do you mean by that?

Michler: I keep trying to make things simpler. The key word is efficiency. A lot of times I use the example of an old air-conditioning unit. It works harder, costs more to keep up, and does less than a new air-conditioning unit. It's not as efficient.

I want my teams to be as efficient as possible. I don't want them to waste effort doing things just to do them. I want every pass and every decision to minimize wasted energy. I want them to pour their energy into doing the things that will increase our chances of winning.

The state championship game was a great example. Our team was very efficient. The players were not tired at the end of that game. They could have kept playing for a long time.

I love teaching people the simplicity of Dutch soccer. I learned the incredible importance of efficiency to the Dutch from my trips to Holland. They have 16 million people living in a country that is a little smaller than twice the state of New Jersey.

The Dutch have to make the most of every inch. They are all about efficiency. All the space in Holland goes up vertically. The architecture makes the absolute most out of every inch. They have bicycle garages like we have car garages. Notice the great efficiency of a bike: no gas, it's comfortable, and it lasts a long time.

The Dutch play the game of soccer with the same focus on efficiency. They are all about making the game as simple as possible. The simple way can be the hardest thing to do most of the time, but, then again, isn't it all about perspective?

There are four keys to improving efficiency: habits, mentality, preparation, and opportunity.

I'm really big on good work habits. I want the players doing things the right way over and over and over. I think this develops a stronger sense of mentality and attention to detail. All of this contributes to efficiency when an opportunity presents itself during a game. They know they are prepared to make the right decisions no matter what situation comes up.

Management Insight

In listening to Terry I landed on the concept of "purposeful efficiency." Peter Drucker made a really interesting statement years ago when he said that great managers are efficient because they do things right and great leaders are effective because they do the right things.

To compete successfully in the midst of today's global competition it is critically important to do the right things in the right way every time.

That's purposeful efficiency.

What is the purpose of your team? What are the right things for your team to do to support that purpose? What are the right ways to do each of those things?

There are no set answers, but if you consistently strive to determine the best answers for your group to each of these questions and implement those answers as well as you can, you will steadily increase the purposeful efficiency of your group.

Coughlin: What is the purpose that your efficient practices and games are geared toward?

Michler: At the beginning of the 2009 season I laid out three goals under a single theme for the players to keep in mind every day. Here they are:

Theme: CBC Soccer – Playing With a Purpose

1. Mental Toughness

    - Improve the ability to overcome minor setbacks.
    - When things don't go exactly right, keep going, take criticism when corrective and constructive, and don't let obstacles (weather, conditions, opponents, referees) get in the way of accomplishing the task.

2. The Attention to Detail

    - Realize the importance of the little things. Little things make a big difference.
    - Develop "mental endurance," which is the ability to focus and concentrate like you never have before.
    - Take nothing for granted and do things the right way all the time.

3. Play in The Right Moment

    - Do the right action at the right time in the right way and to the right place.

Management Insight

What are the specific goals you want your employees to work toward fulfilling every day in an efficient manner?

How will you be able to determine if they are using their time, energy, and resources in a continuously more efficient manner toward fulfilling those objectives?

Beware of Team Destruction

Coughlin: What can ruin a team's performance and has it ever happened to one of your teams?

Michler: That's easy to explain. A "me instead of we attitude" will do it every time. It ruins the team's performance when players have a bad attitude or when every player has to have the ball all of the time.

Whenever you're in anything long enough you get a little bit of everything. Occasionally, very rarely in fact, I've had a group of talented players who got along great everywhere except on the field. I needed 11 soccer balls in every game to keep all of them happy. Unfortunately, there is only one ball.

When that happens you try your best, and then you move on to the next season. Decide whether it's correctable or not. Not every year will be perfect. Don't beat yourself over the head for it. Assess it and correct it if you can. Take it for what it is.

Management Insight

Building a great team takes a lot of intentional effort. Ruining a team can happen very quickly. Be aware of individuals who focus primarily on their personal rewards and recognition.

Assembling very talented employees is powerful, but only if they are working toward the common goals of the team and not just toward their own individual glory and income.

Sustain Your Enthusiasm

Coughlin: How do you maintain your enthusiasm after all these years of dealing with the weather, angry parents, and frustrated fans?

Michler: I've gotten to the point that not too many things affect me. Everybody has their passion. I really love coaching high school soccer. If you can just keep all the negative stuff in perspective and know that it's part of the role, then you can handle it pretty well.

You don't have to accept the verbal stuff people are dumping on you. If you accept it, then you have to deal with it. If you don't accept it, then you don't have to deal with it. I used to teach a Health Class here. I talked a lot about self-esteem and how important it is to deal with negative stuff by not accepting it.

The keys really are to avoid distractions and focus on the game, the team, and the individual players.

Management Insight

Are you doing what you are passionate about doing? Do you see a clear purpose for your work? Do you really buy into that purpose? Are you capable of not accepting negative garbage that people throw at you?

These questions have a lot to do with how long you will be able to maintain your enthusiasm.

De-stress Players

Coughlin: Are your players ever under too much pressure? You've mentioned the importance of not yelling out instructions to players during the game. Why do you not do that?

Michler: Sometimes a results-driven player is under too much pressure from other people and that can get in the way of a great performance.

Occasionally a player's dad or brother will constantly hound him to score more goals and do more things on the field. When that happens I pull the player aside and just ask him how he's doing. Eventually the player usually confides in me what is happening.

Then I tell the player that I really believe in him and that the results will eventually come for him, but for now I want him to just relax and have fun. I point out the things he is doing well and tell him not to worry about the other stuff. A lot of times I don't have an answer for the person at all, but as I allow him to talk and really listen to him I can see him becoming much more relaxed.

Players can't perform if they are under too much stress. I want them to be relaxed because soccer requires a lot of mental and physical effort during the game.

In soccer there is so much mental and physical flow that I don't want to interrupt it, and so I don't yell out to the players during the game. I just want them to concentrate and play when the game is happening. Yelling out instructions to the field just disrupts their concentration and increases their stress.

Management Insight

When you have a terrific employee who is performing well below his or her normal standards take some time to sit down with the person in a one-to-one meeting. Patiently allow the person to share the problems with you. Eventually you may help the person to relax and that can create the dynamics for a great performance.

Perspective from Harry Jansen, One of Terry Michler's Mentors

Harry Jansen is a former KNVB (Royal Dutch Soccer Federation) teacher for Dutch coaches. In the summertime Harry and Terry work together to teach the CBC Dutch Touch Soccer Camp.

Coughlin: Harry, tell me about what you see in Terry as a coach?

Jansen: The Dutch soccer coaching process is based on learning in freedom, learning in safety, and learning from dependence to independence with respect for the opinions, possibilities, and abilities of the players. This approach combined with the knowledge and experience about how to do the training and manage his team are characteristics of Terry Michler as a coach.

Players or employees do not need a cold coach. They need a warm coach with social marks of sympathy. Terry is a warm coach with passion. He is intelligent and is always busy with the individual development of the players. In soccer 11 players make four lines and the four lines make a team. This is a process, and Terry controls this process very well.

A main task of a coach or manager is to create the conditions for the players or employees to do their job and give them the chance to develop themselves.

Without any self-interest Terry always creates these conditions for the players, and the players appreciate his input. Terry works with an open mind and is a good listener.

I was very surprised that Terry knew a lot about the Dutch soccer philosophy when I first him. For me it was clear that Terry was very interested in learning from my knowledge and experience about the coaching of the Dutch soccer style. I was impressed by his quiet way of talking about this item, with his experience with the Dutch training methods, and with the way he was always respectful of my opinion.

From that moment on we have been in a continuous process of thinking, talking, and developing our mutual knowledge about soccer. He has knowledge and experience, but moreover he is a people manager/coach. That makes him successful as a coach. He is a jewel for the development of American soccer.

Management Insight

Technical knowledge and experience are important, but just as important is the ability to build relationships with employees. Do your employees believe that you care about them and their success as individuals in addition to your caring about the results they produce as a team?

Patiently Generate Victories

Coughlin: What role does patience play in the building of a great team?

Michler: Patience is huge in building a great team. That's more so today than ever before. I'm more conscious of what I'm going to say before I say it.

I always try to take my time, gather my thoughts, a. in a way that my players can hear them. 30 years ag have been all over them.

Management Insight

Patience is a critical driver of great long-term team results. Take your time in preparing what you will say to your employees, customers, and shareholders. Reflecting on what you are going to say first and then saying it can dramatically improve results.

Search for Mental Toughness

Coughlin: Are intensity, toughness, tenacity, and aggressiveness important ingredients in being a great player?

Michler: Mental toughness may be the single most important ingredient because there are too many distractions that can get in the way and interfere with maximizing potential. The truly great player has a single-mindedness of purpose that does not allow him to be knocked off his course of action.

All the ingredients you asked about are both physical and mental. I am a big believer that the mental aspect is the most important. The will and determination that drives people toward achieving greatness may be exemplified through physical action, but the mental part is the driving force.

You can readily determine the physical component through visual observation, but it may take a trained eye to observe the finer points of mental toughness and intensity. Truly great players know that losing is part of the deal, but they exhaust all means possible to prevent that from happening.

The deciding factor when all things are equal usually comes down to the player with the stronger mental make-up. Can you really fight through all the obstacles, stay focused, not get too high or too low, and be at your best even when things are not going your way?

The really great players can always find a way to get it done even though it may be with less style points on some occasions. When the final score matters they will be the ones with the best chance to win.

Management Insight

Notice Terry's emphasis on mental toughness over physical toughness. Toughness is not about being macho and screaming at people. It's about staying focused over the long term and doing what you can to guide the project to a successful conclusion.

Look for employees with the mental toughness to persevere and help other people persevere through all the obstacles that stand in the way of success. Individuals in business who take shortcuts in order to avoid difficult situations end up ruining their organization's results.

Know the Defining Moments

Coughlin: What have been the defining moments in your career? What did you learn from those defining moments?

Michler: When I was in eighth grade one of my teachers encouraged me to go to CBC High School. I had never really thought of it before that moment, but after she said that this is where I wanted to go. When I graduated from high school I knew I wanted to come back and teach and coach at CBC.

When I graduated from Rockhurst College I had a chance to go back to CBC and coach the "B" soccer team, but I passed. I had just signed a contract to play professional soccer for the Kansas City Spurs, and I felt I had to give that a try.

When I played professional soccer for two years I was one of only two Americans on the team. I learned a lot from spending time with players from all over the world. That really broadened my perspective on soccer.

Two years later I was called again to come back to CBC, except this time I was asked to be the varsity head coach. The Kansas City Spurs had folded, and I practically ran back. I couldn't wait to start.

Another defining moment was in 1997 when I received the opportunity to go to Holland for a 10-Day Coaching Symposium, which I talked about earlier.

If you never try anything new, when are you going to move forward? You have to move forward at some point. The older I get the more I'm convinced everything happens for a reason. I always stay open to the possibility that I'm going to learn from someone.

Management Insight

Know your defining moments and be prepared to learn from them. Be open to the moment. You don't know when a regular moment will become a defining moment in your life.

Be willing to try something new in order to move forward. At the age of 50 Terry got a chance to travel to Holland to learn from world-class coaches, and that moment changed his life.

Oversee the Organization

Coughlin: At CBC you have five different soccer teams: a varsity, junior varsity, "B" team for sophomores, and a "C" and "D" team for freshmen. How do you oversee the entire soccer organization? How do you incorporate input from your varsity assistant coach, Tom Farishon?

Michler: Over the years we have established a club "culture." Every club does this whether it realizes it or not. The "culture" becomes your trademark, what you are known for, and with that comes certain expectations. Our players understand that, the coaches understand that, and it's passed through the ranks.

I gain insights from all the coaches through communication! I set certain parameters, make time to observe, and encourage consistency within the program to produce the same "goods".

Management Insight

See the importance of culture and communication.

What is your organization's culture? What is it known for? Is the culture you have now effective in producing the desired results? If not, what changes need to be made?

The best assistant is somewhat opposite of yourself so that you have to think and consider different alternatives. Tom and I talk and argue points and then decide the best approach to take.

Perspective from Tom Farishon, CBC High School, Varsity Assistant Soccer Coach

Tom Farishon has been Terry Michler's varsity assistant soccer coach for 24 years. Along the way they have won four state championships and more than 400 games. I asked Tom for his thoughts on Terry's approach to coaching and how they work together.

Tom Farishon: Terry has a great deal of appreciation for details, and I have really learned that these things can make a huge difference in the long run. I think we both help each other with little things that need to be done. Terry and I sit down and discuss players, tactics etc. He listens to what I have to say, I listen to him, and then we try to make the best decision for the team. The final decision is always his call.

My role at practice is to make sure we have the necessary equipment and everything is set up as it should be. Both of us then observe during practice and point out things we need to address. He gives me some freedom to address certain issues.

Terry has such a vast array of drills and an explanation for what each drill does in the big picture that there is always something to learn. His relentless pursuit of perfection keeps everyone on their toes. Terry and I both believe that training is the foundation of what you do on the field in games.

His ability to come up with a drill or to make adjustments to drills or game situations always amazes me. He is constantly putting players under pressure in every way possible and making them work their way out of it. Terry usually does not give answers to situations, but instead he asks questions with the objective being for the players to figure it out on their own.

This helps them to understand the situations themselves. Then when given that situation again in a real game they will hopefully use what they learned in practice.

My role during the game is to observe and comment on things that I see happening on the field. I take an active part in the adjustments that need to be made, but the final decision is his.

Terry could very well be a psychologist. He has tremendous insight into human nature. He addresses problems in a direct and calm manner and allows the players to have their say if he thinks the situation warrants it.

He has the ability to see ten minutes down the line in a game, anticipate what is going to happen, and make whatever adjustments are necessary. He reminds me of John Wooden when he coached at UCLA. He has a great vision of what is coming up.

Terry's approach to the state tournament is pretty much the same as it is during the regular season. We tell the players that if they play every game like it is the state championship then when they get to that game they have played it 33 times already. He will allow some time for recovery as we approach the end of a long and grueling season.

When Terry and I disagree we sit down and discuss our differences and try to come to some type of agreement. If we cannot agree, I realize that he has to make the decision and I have to support him in whatever he decides. We leave our discussions as a united front.

Management Insight

To achieve extraordinary results, it helps to have complementary leadership styles at the top of the organization. It's very important to have a clear number one executive and a clear number two executive. Each individual needs to understand his or her role, embrace that role, and fulfill that role as well as he or she can.

Change the Flow of a Game and a Season

Coughlin: Since soccer is a continuous game of non-stop action with no timeouts how do you affect the flow of a game when it is going in the wrong direction? In a bigger picture, how do you affect the flow of a season when your team is in a slump?

Michler: During an individual game the key is to deliver communication through subs with strategic instructions to try to "mend the fences." Yelling out to the field during a game only disrupts the mental and physical flow of the game.

However, a more effective way to change the flow of a game is to rehearse different options during the training sessions. Always have more than just plan A. That way the players know before the game starts what to do if certain situations occur.

When our team is in a slump for several games during a season the keys to affecting that trend include providing clear communication, holding team meetings, giving the players specific data, making plans, implementing changes, which are sometimes radical changes, and occasionally developing a new approach. Sometimes a day or two off does wonders as well.

> *Management Insight*
>
> Yelling out instructions to your employees during a bad customer meeting is only going to make matters worse. Either communicate a key message to one employee during a break, or have several well-rehearsed options your employees can turn to during the meeting.
>
> When your group is in an extended slump during the course of a year clearly communicate relevant data and be willing to make significant changes.

Chapter Six

Regular Season Tournaments

During the course of the regular season, CBC plays in three tournaments.

For businesses, "regular season tournaments" are the special times during the year when the employees have to be ready to raise their level of performance. These include special sales events or new promotions or new product rollouts.

Avoid Arrogance

Coughlin: I define arrogance as a person who thinks he or she has all the answers and has nothing left to learn from anyone else. With all of the success that you and your players have had over the years, how do you as an individual and your team as a whole avoid arrogance during the regular season tournaments?

Michler: Arrogance is never even a distant thought for us because we're constantly faced with the reality that we can lose our next game. The focus is on the game at hand, and then immediately after that game it's on the next game. Only when everything is said and done do we have time to enjoy what we did. We carry a huge bull's eye on our backs, and we know that every team wants the recognition for beating us. We don't want the repercussions.

The motivation to stay focused replaces any hint of arrogance. Our goals are lofty and if our potential is high then the reality is we are just doing what we should be doing and that does not beget arrogance. As coaches we are constantly reminding the boys to stay focused, be ready for the next opponent, and not drop their guard.

Every score hits the papers the very next morning, and word travels fast. It only takes one mishap to fully realize the extent of the repercussions and the endless questioning about what went wrong and how and why we lost.

Management Insight

Avoid arrogance at all costs. If you are the best in your industry, you cannot afford to be arrogant because everyone is working to beat you. If you are not the best in the industry, you don't deserve to be arrogant.

Win the First Game

Coughlin: What can your team learn from a tournament?

Michler: Tournament play is geared to winning the last game. I preach "win the first game of the tournament." My reasoning is that this puts you in a position to win the tournament. The momentum is with you, and you can use the momentum to carry the team into the next game. To me momentum beats pressure.

Winning builds confidence, and losing tends to compromise confidence. In a tournament there may not be time to recover from a setback. The goals in tournament play are to stay alive, play one game at a time, get to the final game, and win it!

We have hosted the CBC Tournament for more than 30 years in the early part of September. We play a three-game round robin style against three of our biggest and strongest rivals. It tells us early on where we stand and where we might need to improve. Since we host this tournament we take special pride in doing our best to win it, and we have done so nearly 20 times to date.

Following this we play in the prestigious CYC Tournament, which has been in St. Louis for over 50 years. This is a pool play tournament to begin with, and then there are knock-out rounds. This is a grueling week where you must win five games in six days to become champions.

This is a real test of our team's depth and the final rounds resemble the state tournament format with the semi-finals and finals within 24 hours of each other. We use this as a mental approach to prepare for the state tournament.

The final tournament is the Gateway Classic, which brings teams in from across the country. The beauty of this tournament is we get to play teams that we may not have seen before and have to adapt our game to the demands of each opponent. It is a real challenge to adjust to different teams and different styles, but it provides a great learning experience for the players.

Management Insight

Use special occasions during the year to prepare your team for greater challenges later in the year. If your organization is in retail sales, a one-day sales promotion in April can help your team learn what needs to be improved on before the rush of the Christmas season.

Understand the Difference with the State Tournament

Coughlin: In what ways is a regular-season tournament different from the state tournament at the end of the season?

Michler: The biggest difference is that the end-of-the-season tournament has more lasting results. Lose and turn in your uniforms; win and stay in the hunt for the big prize. Win the whole enchilada, and you have lasting memories for a lifetime.

The big tournament only comes along once a year, and for the seniors there is no next year. The consequence for the seniors is serious. Many players have prepared themselves for several years to have a chance to be a state champion.

Management Insight

Significant events throughout the course of the year help to raise the performance bar of your organization. Use each one of them to help guide your organization to be better prepared for your ultimate challenge whatever that may be for your business.

Discover the Heart of Your Team

Coughlin: What do you discover about the heart of your team during a regular-season tournament?

Michler: Every tournament that we play in has a different format. Players have to adapt to the different demands and find a way to win. The bottom line is you find out which players "step up" when the pressure is on. Tournament play is a pressure-packed event. Only two teams get to the last game, and only one team wins the trophy. You find out who will help you in the biggest games at the end of the year.

Any mistake could jeopardize your chances to advance. The schedule of games is very demanding so mental focus and physical energy become key factors.

Management Insight

As your work team takes on a special event look for those individuals who flourish under pressure and search for people who do not want this type of situation. This will help you to determine which individuals should play key roles in guiding your business at critical moments in the year's biggest projects.

Chapter Seven

State Tournament

The state tournament represents the greatest challenge of all.

In your business, what is the single greatest test your team faces? That is your state tournament. That is what brings out the very best in you and your group.

Perspective from Mike Gauvain, One of Terry Michler's Top Opposing Coaches

Mike Gauvain has a unique perspective on Terry Michler.

For 22 years he has coached against Terry. Mike, known as "Vader," is the head soccer coach at Chaminade High School in St. Louis, Missouri. He has won three Missouri Class 3 Boys High School Soccer State Championships. His coaching record is 430 wins, 137 losses, and 55 ties. He has been to the state Final Four six times, and in 2001 his Chaminade soccer team was voted National High School Champions by Adidas and NSCAA.

He has also coached boys and girls club teams that have won national championships with J.B. Marine and Scott Gallagher. As one of the top forwards in the country he played against Terry Michler's CBC teams for three seasons when he was in high school.

Mike is also the co-owner with his wife, Theresa, of JJ Twig's Pizza & Pub, which serves one of the best pizzas in St. Louis and is one of Terry's favorite places to eat. I sat down with Mike and Terry at JJ Twig's to gain Mike's insights on Terry's coaching approaches. Our conversation covered not only soccer topics, but also how Mike uses lessons from coaching high school soccer as a small business owner.

Mike Gauvain: I have known of Terry since 1976 when I played for St. Mary's High School. I didn't really know him then, but I admired him. My high school coach, Steve Bettlach, warned our team that Mr. Michler's CBC teams would always be extremely well prepared, and he was right. They were well prepared.

When I went to college my coach, Bob Guelker, also talked about how Terry had his teams extremely well prepared.

What I've come to learn is that Terry prepares his players as student/athletes and not just as soccer players. In high school sports you're dealing with the whole person, not just the athlete. That is something I've learned as a coach as well. You have to be prepared to treat each player as an individual person, not just as a soccer player. Terry does a great job at that.

Management Insight

As a manager, you're not dealing with the individual as just a skilled employee. You're really dealing with the whole person. Be prepared as much as you can for business issues, but also keep in mind you need to be prepared for non-business issues to pop up as well.

Gauvain: I was only 25 when I became the head soccer coach at Chaminade. I was nervous and young. We only won six games that first year. I didn't go to Terry for advice because I was young, and I thought I knew everything about coaching. I was also a little intimidated. We lost 9-0 one game to another team, and I actually thought about quitting coaching.

Then I went to watch CBC play, and I saw how they had a consistent style of play. I noticed how Terry would give good players a chance to perform in the big games regardless of their size, age, or year in school. That really made an impact on me. I noticed how players who got playing time as freshmen ended up as juniors and seniors making everyone around them better.

By my third year I had freshmen playing key starting positions for my team, and within a few more years we were competing well with CBC on a regular basis.

We actually beat CBC in pool play of a tournament in my third season. I was so nervous to shake Terry's hand because I didn't know what to say. My team went on to lose the next two games, and Terry's team won the tournament championship.

Michler: On our team this year we had a senior who dominated the entire middle of the field. He played on the varsity as a freshman, but he was a small, skinny kid back then. I kept him because he had a great soccer brain. Part of coaching insight is to know which player to give an opportunity to move up early in his career. You have to be able to look into the future and predict which players will be the leaders two to three years from now.

Gauvain: It's the same way with my pizza business. Three years ago we hired a young guy and told him he was going to be the dishwasher. We also told him we would teach him how to make the pizzas. Now he's one of our best pizza makers and one of our most valuable employees.

Right away he showed his willingness to work hard and to learn fast. In the beginning we let him stand by the employees making the pizzas, and gradually we worked him into that role. Just like in soccer we want to perform consistently well all of the time. One way to do that is to groom future leaders.

You don't want freshmen to fail when you put them in a varsity game at a crucial moment. You guide them along and little by little you increase their responsibilities until they are ready.

Management Insight

Look into the future. Which of your employees will you be willing to give an early chance to perform in a critically important position? Who are going to be the leaders in your organization in three years?

Coughlin: What ultimately brought you two together as such great coaching friends?

Gauvain: As a coach I saw how prepared CBC was and I wanted my team to be more like that. I wanted us to play the same consistent style of play that CBC played. I definitely started changing the way I ran my practices after I spent more time with Terry. After a few years I started scouting my opponents and taking more notes at those games because I noticed that Terry was doing it.

Michler: You gravitate toward people who share the same kind of philosophy toward the game that you have. Another thing is I want the other coach to know when I saw him do something really well or saw his players do something really well. Whether we won or lost, I will go over to the other coach after the game and tell him when I saw something really good that happened. Sometimes I will go over to the other team and let them know I saw something that they did really well.

Mike and I have a great friendly rivalry. We want to compete against each other. That's the most fun part of sports.

Gauvain: In 1998 in the state semifinals we beat CBC on penalty kicks after four overtimes. That was a thrilling game. Both teams poured everything they had into that game.

Terry and I respect each other. One year he gave me some advice right before my team played in the state finals. He had notes on the other team, and he gave me everything he knew about them. That was really helpful. That's the kind of friendship we have.

When we compete we both want to win very badly, but we respect each other and we keep the whole thing in perspective. We remember it's just a game. We are competing in soccer and we are competing to get the same players, but we keep it in perspective.

In business, it's a little harder because that's your livelihood. I don't share ideas with my competitors as much as I do with other soccer coaches, but I do respect my competitors. My wife and I will have dinner at a competitor across the street, and that competitor will bring his team over to JJ Twig's for a meal. It is a little different in business, but I do try to be respectful of my competitors. No one wants to see anyone fail.

Management Insight

A sport is not a perfect analogy for a business. One really is just a game, and the other is the livelihood for a lot of people. However, you can still respect your competitor and learn from your competitor and at times even support your competitor.

Coughlin: Mike, what have you learned from Terry about how to succeed in the state tournament?

Gauvain: If you win the state quarterfinals game, you get a week to prepare for the Final Four. Some people think that's too long, but I completely disagree. If you are fortunate to get there, it's the best week of the year. As I said, Terry has taught me a lot about the importance of preparation. That's my favorite part.

The buildup is exciting at school and throughout the community. The buzz is building, but the best part for me is preparing my team. My whole mindset during that week is to get the players to focus on doing what they do well. We may tweak a few things, but we're not going to change a lot. We want to keep everything sharp and focused.

Michler: Before each state championship game I always tell my players the same thing. I'll say, "Now it's your turn. Just relax, go out there, and have fun."

I've seen too many teams in the state championship game get so intense that they can't play their best soccer. The players have to relax, and it's the coach's job to help them relax.

Gauvain: We've been to the state championship game six times and have won three of them. I tell the players, "This is a big game. This is a big moment. Go out there and enjoy the moment. You worked all season for this moment so enjoy it."

> *Management Insight*
>
> How are you getting your employees to relax before a big moment? If you press them too hard, you may end up hurting your business results a great deal. If you have prepared them well over the long term, then try to loosen them up as they head into a critical business juncture.

Michler: Mike, how much coaching experience do you bring to your business?

Gauvain: A ton. Some people will get really panicked in a busy moment in our restaurant. Just like in soccer, I try to get them to take a second to find a solution. Sometimes you have to make a quick decision in business, but the same is true in soccer.

When you're down by a goal with 15 minutes left in the game you have to decide if you are going to move two defenders into the midfield. You don't have an hour to make up your mind.

That happens in business a lot. If the players or employees see you staying calm, then they can stay calm. I'll give you an example. Five customers came in here the other night, ordered a pizza with five toppings, and were upset with the bill. They said, "The Specialty Pizza price is different than what we're being charged for."

I said, "You're right. You changed three of the toppings so it's no longer the Specialty Pizza. So it costs more. It says it right here on the menu that you can't change the items and still get that price." They said, "Well, you should have put that in bold on the menu."

They were really upset, but I just stayed calm. One person sarcastically said to me, "So what are you going to do about it?" I finally said to them, "You understand how the pricing works now, right?" They said, "Yeah, we get it." Then I said, "I'll tell you what. I'll give you the Specialty Pizza price this time." They thanked me over and over.

You know what the difference was between the two prices? Four dollars. If I stay calm, then maybe my team at JJ Twig's will stay calm. It's the same way in soccer. Sometimes players get really frazzled when they sit on the bench for awhile. So I will say to them, "When you get back in there, I just want you to focus on these couple of things. So just relax, get a drink of water, get yourself mentally ready, and I'll get you back in there."

Now sometimes I need to be really firm with players and employees. Sometimes I say, "You just can't do those things. It's detrimental to the team." One time we had a key employee who changed the sauce for our pizzas because he wanted it to taste differently. I told him, "You just can't do that." Ultimately we had to let him go for a variety of reasons. Players need to perform within the framework that I choose.

Management Insight

As Terry says, a big part of your job as a manager is to see the big picture and then narrow your focus to the smaller picture within the bigger one. Stay calm and resolve the small items that could ultimately hurt the big picture.

Gauvain: One challenge I have in soccer and in business is when players and employees think they are very, very, very good when in reality they aren't. One of my biggest challenges in coaching is deciding when to move a sophomore up to the varsity team. Sometimes I've cut a sophomore, and he has transferred.

This type of player acts like we won't be able to survive without him. That happens sometimes with our employees. An employee will leave and act like we won't be able to keep the business open. Both players and employees can overestimate how good they really are at what they do.

However, I do sometimes give in to a player's suggestion at a practice or an employee's suggestion at work. I want them to know we listen to their ideas and we consider their ideas. One thing I'm proud of is I'm approachable.

People here at JJ Twig's know that Theresa and I are the bosses and that they can come to us with their ideas. At school the players know that I'm in charge and I'm willing to give them some freedom. I want to create an environment where people can do their jobs without me hanging all over them. Also, our employees see Theresa and me working in the restaurants. We're not just sitting around. That helps to set the tone for everyone.

Management Insight

Management is an art, not a science. Just as soccer coaches need to use a variety of approaches to bring out the best in their teams, so too do business managers.

Work to understand when you need to be firm, when you need to be flexible, and when you need to model hard work.

Pursue the Dream

Coughlin: What role does having a compelling dream play in building a great team?

Michler: The dream for any season is part of the common goal we all share. The goal for all of my teams has been to win the state championship. Every year we want to add another star to the uniform. The more mature the team is, the more we talk about the dream. If the group is not that mature, then I only talk about the dream occasionally and in more of an indirect way.

This year's team was very mature. I told them, "I'm demanding more of you because of what we're capable of. If I don't demand more of you, then I will fail at my responsibilities." With this year's team, if I had told them they could have a day off from practice, they would say, "That's fine. Leave us the soccer balls so we can practice on our own."

It's all about managing performance in relation to expectations, having a core plan, and allowing for some leeway as is necessary. Then develop the plan over time through repeated practice with careful observation never far off.

Management Insight

Great teams have dreams, especially barrier-breaking dreams. What is your group going after? What is it that will get the juices flowing and keep the flame of passion alive?

Even if you've been with your group for a long time it's still important to set realistic and barrier-breaking goals to spur your group on.

Lean on Your Experience

Coughlin: In your book, *Dutch Total Football*, you talked about the importance of insight. What does the word "insight" mean to you, why is it so important, and how do you gain it?

Michler: Insight is how you see something unfold whether it's in relationships, on the field, or within the team. Insight affects a person's perspective, mentality, and behaviors. If you look at a situation for what it really is rather than for what you want it to be, you will see it very differently.

I really think I look at things differently than most people. Experience lends itself to improved insight. I'll give you an example. In the state quarterfinal game we were playing the next highest rated team in the state behind us. We had already played them three times during the season without a loss.

It's very hard to beat a team four times in a row. In those three games they only scored one goal against us. They had the most experienced team of anyone in the state. Several of their starters were starters for three years.

I had four days to get the team ready for that game. I had an insight based on my experience that what we needed to win was a tougher mindset. I felt we were going to be in for a very tough game. When you have experience in a situation you fall back on the realization that you've been here before and know what you need to do.

Instead of practicing the boys a lot and going over a lot of soccer stuff, I decided we needed to focus in on the idea of "The Will of a Champion." I wanted the players to concentrate on having stronger confidence and mental toughness.

I showed the team videotapes of the great Liverpool teams in the late seventies and early eighties. Then I showed them a tape of the 2005 Liverpool – AC Milan Champions League Final. Liverpool was down 3-0 at halftime, but fought back to win 4-3.

I wanted the boys to see the importance of having the will to win no matter what happened in the quarterfinal game. Our theme was "stay in the game." They saw and heard from the champions what it took to win. We only practiced soccer for 20 minutes on each of the practice days. We spent the vast majority of our time watching videos of great teams.

With 10 minutes left in the game the other team scored a goal and went ahead of us, but our team responded right away and tied the game. During the five-minute break before overtime started, I said to the boys, "Remember the will of a champion. Visualize yourself doing whatever it takes to win this game."

That's exactly what they did. We won in overtime. How did I have the insight that this particular game was going to come down to mental toughness more than soccer ability? Experience.

Michler: To get ready for the state semi-finals and finals, I felt we needed to change things up. I felt we needed to focus on playing better. Everything we did in the three practices leading up to the last two games was focused on quick passing and going to goal. Insight comes from thinking before you do something. Ask yourself, "What does this situation call for?"

Management Insight

Lean on your experience to help you see what might unfold and what you will need to do to be effective in the new situation.

Before you march into any one of the many meetings you have every day, step back and ask yourself, "What does this situation call for?"

Perspective from Drew Duncan, One of the Captains on Terry Michler's 2009 State Championship Team

Drew Duncan was a four-year goalkeeper on the CBC Varsity Team. As a senior, he was All-State First Team. I asked Drew for his thoughts on Terry Michler.

Drew Duncan: I've played soccer for 13 years. Mr. Michler has influenced my approach to practices by saying that everything is done for a reason and you need to get something out of everything you do in practice. He is an effective coach during practices because he wants everything done to perfection. Every pass, every touch, every shot, and every idea needs to be perfect.

Mr. Michler is so effective during the state tournament because he has a lot of experience. He knows how to get his teams ready, and he knows what to tell his team and what not to tell his team.

The quarter-final game was an amazing game. It was the state final pretty much because it was the two best teams playing in a state final atmosphere. It was a battle between the two best teams going back and forth the whole game.

We went down 1-0 with about ten minutes left so I'm sure we all got a little worried. About three minutes later Austin Tierney played a free kick into the box, and Sam Carenza won the head ball and got the game-tying goal that took us to overtime.

During the time we had to talk, Mr. Michler talked about the will of a champion, which we spent most of the week before the game talking about. Basically it means that no matter what happens a champion always finds a way to win.

The overtime started just how the whole game went with back and forth play from both teams. Then Kyle Malle played the ball to Austin. He worked it to the end line and played the ball across to Justin Bilyeu, who hammered it home, and we all went crazy!

Visualize Success

Coughlin: When you are heading into a state tournament and while you are playing in that three-week tournament how do you help your players visualize being successful?

Michler: I always reinforce in my players that they chose to go to CBC for many reasons, but playing in the biggest games of the year is always one of the top reasons.

The end-of-the-year tournament draws the biggest crowds and leaves the most lasting impression. This is the time of the year that you want to be playing and hopefully playing your best! The entire season is geared to this tournament for all the teams from the wishful thinkers to the real contenders.

We mentally go back to the hot days of August when training began, and we talk about the sweat and hard work that went into preparing the mind and the body for this moment. We explain how the state tournament is the culmination of the process of building momentum day by day from a myriad of experiences, all preparing for this moment.

I tell a story of how little kids go to those state championship games and leave very inspired after watching the players. I tell the boys that they were that little kid who came out to those same games. I say, "Now it's your turn to inspire those young kids just like you were inspired years ago." I usually get pretty emotional when telling this to the boys, and they like it.

Management Insight

Remind your employees they came to your organization to take on big challenges and to make an extraordinary impact. Tell them it's their turn to have fun making a difference in the world.

Perspective from Chris Lawson, One of Terry Michler's Top Opposing Coaches

Chris Lawson is the head soccer coach at Rockhurst High School in Kansas City, Missouri, and one of Terry's biggest competitors for the state championship each year. His team has won the Missouri Class 3 Boys High School Soccer State Championship four times and made it the Final Four 12 consecutive times. He is also one of Terry's biggest fans.

Coughlin: How have you gotten to know Terry over the years?

Lawson: I've known Terry since I started coaching at Rockhurst High School in 1994. We became better friends over time and have a great mutual respect for each other.

Most know Terry as a great coach, but he is also a true gentleman, friend, and mentor to a lot of coaches. When I come to St. Louis he will meet up with my family and try to get together for breakfast or lunch. My son, Owen, and Terry's grandkids have met up before to swim when I stay in the St. Louis area. He is a patient grandpa.

In 2005 Terry took time to come by my dad's 85th birthday in Sedalia on his way back from a coaching clinic in Kansas City. He also came to my dad's funeral in 2007 over the Christmas holidays. He has extended his friendship to me and my family.

We have coached against each other five or six times. In 2004 we lost in triple overtime to CBC in the state final game. We defeated CBC in 2007 and 2008 in the regular season, which gave our team the confidence to go and eventually win the '07 and '08 state championships.

Coughlin: How has Terry influenced your approach to coaching in general?

Lawson: First and foremost, he is passionate about coaching and developing players. It shows in his team's preparation and play.

Terry always talks about developing the whole player so they are technically, tactically, physically, and mentally prepared. He strives to instill those four key pillars in each of his players.

Terry is the consummate professional. Even though he is a great competitor and even if you beat his team, he will level with you and tell you what he likes about your team. He will give you insight on what he thinks your team needs to do to be able to move on and compete for a state title.

There are a lot of great teams around every year, but the hallmark attributes of their style of play and the precision they play with make CBC truly a great program. There is a difference between his teams and the others. They may not win the title annually, but everyone in the state knows regardless of their record you have to beat CBC to get a chance to win a state title.

Year in and year out CBC is consistently there, and that is what makes the program at CBC different from other teams. I have tried to do the same at Rockhurst, and I am sure other coaches strive to have a program as consistent as CBC.

Terry shares his knowledge with other coaches and asks that you share it with others like others have shared their knowledge with him to better the game. It is an educational cycle to improve the quality of play. He reads and analyzes the game extremely well, and his scouting reports are spot on when I seek out information on teams I play in the St. Louis area.

I have used several activities Terry has shared with me. He showed me a great shooting activity after he beat us in the 2004 state final. It was the practice drill that he used to create the game-winning goal. We use it to this day and it is invaluable.

Also, Terry has a great outline he shared with me that allows a coach to know his players psychological make-up better in an effort to maximize each player's output. It is very helpful.

It helps players assess factors that keep them from achieving their best, focus on the factors that improve their quality of play, and identify characteristics they can directly control mentally.

> *Management Insight*
>
> If you want to raise the standard of performance in your organization, share what you know with other managers in your organization. Do it openly and freely.
>
> If you want to raise the standard of performance in your industry, share what you know with other managers outside of your organization.
>
> If you want to raise the standard of performance in the world, share what you know with managers from any industry.

Coughlin: How has he influenced your approach toward conducting practices?

Lawson: We practice in a more efficient manner! He taught me that practicing less often but doing so more economically can be especially useful around playoff time. Most young coaches want to cover too much. Now I am ok with doing a few things really well and not forcing things to take place that are not going well.

Coughlin: How has he influenced your approach toward individual games?

Lawson: When you play Terry he will do things as a coach you may not see much from other coaches. He makes other coaches better because you have to game plan for each game expecting something unique. He will assign a player on his team to mark up your "play maker" and follow him all over the field.

Even when CBC has the ball this player from CBC will still be marking your offensive playmaker. Some players who are not mentally tough enough will get caught up in the emotion of not getting open or being able to get to the ball, and you can see the frustration set in. Terry will employ this if he thinks it will alter the opponent's quality of play. It is vital to have multiple players contributing when you play CBC.

If you have a player that is suspect on one side of the field, Terry may move one of his players to that side to specifically test that player. Some coaches would just have the player on that side test the opponent, but Terry would send a message by moving a wide right mid to the left side if he thought it would work better.

Management Insight

Great managers cause you to improve in order to compete with them. Who is the "Terry Michler" in your organization or industry that brings out the best in you? Seek that person out and improve your performance by trying to perform at a higher level than he or she does.

Coughlin: How has he influenced your approach to individual seasons?

Lawson: Terry will be the first to tell you that he is blessed to have some talented players, but he plays the players who buy into the program and play for the right reasons. Terry allows his players to maintain their individuality within the context of the program. He has some policies and expectations that are non-negotiable, and the great players and teams he has coached know that.

His 2009 state championship team seemed to be very fluid, and Terry liked how they interacted and could change positions or roles and not miss a beat.

I have seen some of his teams where he had 11 great players starting, and then I have seen his state title teams like 2004, 2005, and 2009 that modeled the "11 players that play best together" phrase. They were talented, but you could see they bought into the "team first" mantra.

On years when we are in the Final Four and CBC is out, I will observe Terry sitting in the stands tracking our players' habits and our team's style of play. You have to be well prepared not to be too predictable, or you will meet your match and your team won't be able to adapt when you play CBC the next year.

Coughlin: How has he influenced your approach to player selection?

Lawson: Terry selects players that are talented and can execute their role, but they have to play within the system. He is confident and experienced enough to manage highly talented players coming through his system. He is very careful and very fair when selecting underclassmen to play for CBC.

The technical, tactical, and physical attributes have to be there for a freshman to make it at the varsity level, but Terry will look at the player's emotional and mental maturity as well to see if he can handle that level of play over the course of 30 games over three months.

> *Management Insight*
>
> Detailed and careful selection of personnel goes a long way toward achieving sustainable success in business.

Coughlin: How has he influenced your approach to the style of play that your team uses?

Lawson: Terry's team normally controls the ball more than any of their opponents. When you play them you better employ a strategy that promotes keeping the ball more than CBC, or you will let them dictate the tempo. If you look at soccer teams that are highly successful, you will see certain hallmarks that each incorporate in their training and playing style.

Terry respects Dutch soccer, and the Dutch coaches have influenced his coaching style a great deal. The Dutch have certainly influenced soccer on a world-wide basis and competed well internationally on a consistent basis. His team's possession style with an emphasis on patterns of play and their flair for being able to beat you individually or collectively has made CBC a consistent contender in Missouri and nationally.

I don't know of any other team in the Midwest who play as tough a schedule day in and day out and who consistently contend for a state title in a state that produces some of the best high school talent nationally.

At Rockhurst one of our proudest hallmarks is our style of play in having the ability to possess the ball, which as CBC has shown can not only help the team win more often but also develops players who can play at any and all levels.

Coughlin: How has he influenced your approach to individual players?

Lawson: I remember a young man at CBC named Joe Brennan who scored the game winning goal in 2004 against us in the state championship match. One of the best things about such a tough loss was that Brennan wasn't one of Terry's starters. I suspect Brennan and no one else on the CBC team or staff cared about his stats or the fact he didn't start.

He came off the bench and helped his team win the state title in the third overtime by hitting a "special goal" from 27 yards out. Terry promotes that type of confidence in all of his players.

Terry is a veteran who knows how to get the most out of his players. He is very clear in articulating to each player his role within the scheme of the system. He promotes each player to play within his strengths and value the role he has been given.

Coughlin: How has he influenced your approach to your overall team?

Lawson: It's in how I manage my starters and role players. This is critical in this era where high school players underestimate the value of role players. They emphasize skipping the intermediate stages of development to play right away. I have become a better communicator as a result of having been around Terry.

Management Insight

A special rivalry can generate special performances.

Do you respect your biggest and best competitor? Do you share insights with each other? Do you bring out the best or the worst in each other?

CBC, Chaminade, and Rockhurst have won eight of the last nine Missouri Class 3 Boys High School Soccer State Championships. However, notice the extraordinary respect that Mike Gauvain and Chris Lawson have for Terry Michler.

Coughlin: Are there any specific insights or phrases from Terry that you find yourself incorporating into your way of coaching?

Lawson: I frequently use one of Terry's famous lines about playing efficiently, which is "I have never seen the tongue hang off a soccer ball. Players get tired. The ball doesn't get tired. Let the ball do the work." Terry uses this line to promote passing for possession and make the game simpler.

I use his philosophy of the four pillars of the complete player a lot in our evaluations of players, and as I coach I use it to evaluate myself and our staff to ensure I am always trying to develop the complete player in those four realms (technically, tactically, physically, and mentally). Any successful team I have been a part of has demonstrated mastery of those four pillars.

Everyone in the coaching ranks in our region knows that if you have a weakness and you play a Terry Michler-coached team you better improve upon it or his team will exploit it. Many coaches can see weaknesses, but not all of them can employ tactics or strategy to actually have their players execute against that weakness.

Management Insight

Take out a sheet of paper and write down the greatest strengths of the best managers you have ever worked for or against. Too often we look for what is wrong with the other person rather than looking for what we can learn from them.

Chapter Eight

Beyond Soccer

Four years is not a lot of time.

At most a person gets to play soccer for Terry Michler for four years. However, Terry's impact on many of his players lasts a lifetime.

You may only get a few years with any of your employees, but your impact as a manager can last for their entire careers. What is the legacy you want to leave behind?

Guide Players to the Next Level

Coughlin: You have sent more than 230 of your players on to play college soccer and more than 30 to play professional soccer. How do you guide players to play at the next level?

Michler: I always say there is a place where everyone can play. I use that during tryouts as well. My feeling is that if a player has the desire to play and is willing to dedicate himself, he can find a place where his level is acceptable. Not everyone can play at the highest level, but everyone can play somewhere.

If a player is realistic about his ability level and seeks out a team comparable to his playing level, he will be able to continue playing and enjoying himself. My biggest issue is that I have to balance the desires of the players with the realities of their abilities and their chances for success at the next level. I have to be honest with the next coach and not "sell him a bill of goods."

Most of our players are able to continue playing in college. Over the years our reputation and tradition have helped open doors and provide opportunities, but then it's up to the player to take it from there. My involvement is to advise, make contacts, and get the kids' names in front of college coaches.

It makes me feel good to know that many of our former players have had successful college careers and received their degree as well. Every time you place a kid in a school and he does well, it's easy to go back to that coach and offer another player.

The fact that so many of our players continue playing is a testament to their dedication, passion, and competitiveness.

Management Insight

Once someone has done a great job for you, he or she is one of your players forever.

Don't just help your employees succeed while they are on your team. Help them succeed at every step in their careers including when they have moved on to other organizations.

Connect Soccer to Business

Coughlin: What parallels do you see between a high school soccer team and a business, whether it's a small, medium, or large business?

Michler: In my opinion there are a lot of parallels. They all need organizational plans, motivation, goals, expectations, and action plans. You need to do things the right way through correct repetitions with maximum participation and enjoyment.

Start with the product, perfect the product, and do it so often in the right way that it becomes second nature to do it that way. Our "product" is our performance during the games.

Every organization has a product or service that it needs to perfect by doing things the right way so often that it just becomes second nature for them.

You reach the goal away from the job as much as you do on the job. You have to get away from the work. You can't enjoy it when you are absorbed in it all the time.

un comes from your perspective, which is the way you approach your work. Work has to be fun or otherwise people won't be able to do their best.

In business and in soccer you have to learn to communicate with people. The Dutch are the best traders in the world. They had to learn to speak everyone else's language first because they are such a small country. In school they learn French, English, and German. They speak better English than people in the United States do.

They prepare themselves to be able to communicate with people from lots of different countries. Consequently, there are more Dutch soccer coaches around the world than from anywhere else.

Collaboration is important both in business and in soccer. The 2009 state championship game was at 6 PM on a Saturday. That morning we had a meeting with the players at 10:30. I asked the players, "What do you think is the best way to play tonight? How do you want to play?" I listened to their ideas and took it all in.

Then I said, "Let me show you some ideas I have." We discussed the ideas for awhile and then we landed on the game plan that we stuck to that night. At the end of the meeting, I said, "Are you guys ok with doing it this way?" They said they were. It was a good plan with perfect execution by the players. Here is the diagram I put on the screen for the players to consider:

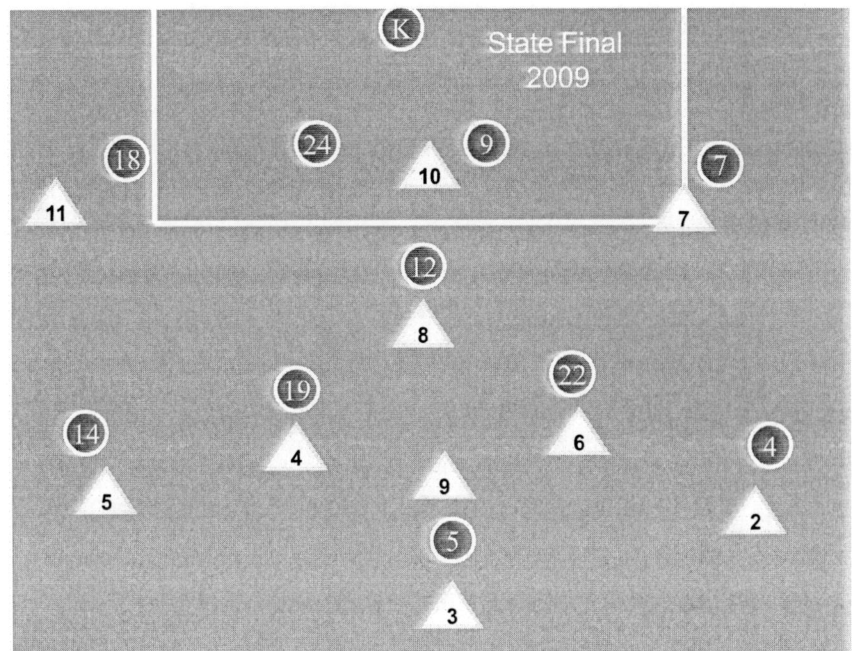

CBC in Triangles, Opponent in Circles

A few days after the championship game I saw a mother of one of the players. She told me her son came home after that meeting and said, “As soon as we walked out of that room I knew we were going to win.”

For me, it was a fulfilling moment to sit back and watch that game. It was the fulfillment of all of my experiences and insights.

Management Insight

Terry Michler's Five Critical Business-Building Ideas:

1. Focus on perfecting whatever it is that you sell.
2. Prepare yourself to be able to communicate with people who have vastly different backgrounds and experiences than you do.
3. Create organizational plans that the members of the group have input in developing.
4. Make sure to keep the work enjoyable.
5. Maximize participation toward improving results.

Coughlin: Have players ever shared with you how a lesson they learned through soccer has application in the business world?

Michler: Absolutely!! The common threads are working hard, believing in yourself, and not giving up.

Perspective from Pat Long, One of Terry Michler's Former Players

Pat Long played on CBC's 1984 state championship team. Since then he has gone into the restaurant business. However, as he explains, he still carries Terry's ideas with him. I asked him to share his thoughts on Terry Michler.

Pat Long: To say the least Terry has influenced things in my life. It's funny to me now how much of an impact he has had as I surely didn't see it that way when I was in my teens.

I have two daughters who recently asked me as part of a school assignment which individuals had the biggest influence on my life. I told them that along with my father Terry Michler was the biggest influence. They asked why I felt that way.

I told them that during my senior year in high school I almost gave up on myself completely. I was never a good student primarily because I didn't put in the effort. I was questioned by several teachers about being lazy, spoiled, and not driven in any way. Their criticism was the last thing I needed. I was merely young, confused, and insecure.

I decided to quit the soccer team and take the path of least resistance. This seemed the right way to get out of the firing line. I hadn't quit because I was unhappy with my role on the team. It was quite the opposite. I quit out of shame and a total lack of belief in myself. After a call from Terry I decided to give it another try.

I went on to have a senior soccer year that would be one of the best years of my life. Coach Michler put me in a position to succeed and treated me in a way few others had. To this day that season helps set the tempo for the way I handle myself on a daily basis. That year he gave me self-belief and rekindled my love for the game that would continue throughout that year. I know now that it happened because of his qualities as a coach.

I dread to think of how things would have turned out if I had not had that senior year under his influence. It gave me a year to treasure and helped me shed many self-doubts. While many challenges followed I had the strength to battle because of him and that year. I think of it often.

All the wins mean a lot, but I thought you would like to know about Terry Michler's long-term influence on his players. I for one will never forget it.

I'm in the restaurant business now and there are a lot of parallels to coaching. One of the things that Terry instilled in me was holding people to a high standard. While those are simply words, Terry taught me through his actions how to help every individual reach his potential through a mix of discipline and personal attention.

If we weren't working our hardest or made some unacceptable mistakes, Terry would let us know or yank us from the game. However, he did it in a way that let you retain your self-esteem and build upon the belief you had in your inherent skill.

I remember one specific example. We were playing our hated rivals, and we were winning 4-0. On a punt from their goalie I back-headed the ball into our own net, which spoiled the shutout. Terry pulled me from the game and sat me for about 15 minutes.

He then put me back in, and I immediately had an assist on our next goal. While this may seem like a natural move to any coach, it was the way Terry handled our day-to-day training that let me know he could be disappointed in my actions, but still believed in me enough to go right back to me when it counted.

I also recall three or four small talks I had with Terry that stick with me to this day. Somehow he knew exactly when I needed his advice. I think he watched our lives when we didn't even know he was watching. For me the high school years were the toughest years of my life. I felt like no authority figures truly cared for me as an individual, except for Terry.

He was his own man. He stood apart in his approach to the young men. He was then and is now a man of few words. Yet when he did speak those words had real meaning, and you knew where you stood with him.

I believe that is the key place where he had an effect on the way I operate my business. My employees know where they stand with me. I am involved with them as people, not just employees.

I know what makes all of them tick, and I do my best to help them continually grow as people.

At times that means I know they are going to grow out of working for me, but if I show them respect I know my company will benefit because my employees will feel good about themselves and the place where they work. They know I'll hold them to a high standard, but I'll do it in a way that lets them know that I believe in them as individuals.

> *Management Insight*
>
> Your legacy as a manager is not completely summarized by the P&L Statement. Beyond earning money and taking care of your family, the greatest aspect of being a business manager is the impact you have on other people's lives.
>
> You may never know the difference you will make in other people's lives. However, manage in a way that 25 years from now someone might still be using what you taught them to generate better sustainable results.

Reinforce Lessons for Life

Coughlin: Terry, as you think about ideas that last beyond soccer what comes to mind?

Michler: Soccer is a vehicle to teach valuable life lessons. In the daily action of preparing the team I think a soccer coach teaches lessons for life. It's usually done more informally than formally. You teach the ideas, and you know they will stay with the players after their soccer careers are over. Many times it comes down to what you allow or don't allow.

A lot of people are content with being mediocre. What is average for our team would be a spectacular result for other teams. We have to work really hard just to have an average season. Until I retire, there is always a next game. I live in a "Yea, but..." world. We're judged on our last game and our next game. That helps me to stay grounded. There is nothing worse than being sky high one day and extremely low the next.

Having said that, I think there are five keys for any group to win. They are talent, effort, chemistry, coaching, and luck.

Talent is the basis for long-term success. Who can play? Who has the ability to do what is needed in your organization? Talent is having the capacity to perform under pressure and the ability to create and capitalize.

Effort is both physical and mental. Physical effort comes down to practicing hard and playing hard. It means going after the opportunity, pressuring the opponent, and denying the opponent opportunities to beat you. Mental effort is about determination and being ready to perform. It includes maintaining very high concentration, intensity, and confidence.

Chemistry is the critical ingredient. It means team unity and togetherness where the members of the group provide positive support to one another.

Usually you generate your own luck. The harder you work, the luckier you get. If you wait for good things to happen with your hand out, good things are not likely to happen.

Coaching brings it all together. It binds the group together and encourages the chemistry. I think it's really important to know the individuals in the group as much as possible so you know what will work and what won't work.

These five things have to integrate for a group to be really successful.

It's not like five separate blocks that you can put on top of each other. You can have a boatload of one of them, but not enough of another. You have to have all five. The intangibles have to come together in order for the group to be successful.

> *Management Insight*
>
> How can you improve and integrate the talent, effort, chemistry, coaching, and luck in your organization?

Perspective from Austin Tierney, One of the Captains on Terry Michler's 2009 State Championship Team

Austin Tierney was a four-year varsity soccer player at CBC. His senior year he was named First-Team All State and First-Team All-American. His thoughts on Terry Michler sum up several of the key points in this book.

Austin Tierney: Coach Michler influenced my approach to practice in a monumental way. He made me a true believer that the way you practice will directly affect your game on the pitch. Putting the right amount of effort into practice and doing things the correct way will make you improve as a player.

I personally have a yearning for practice ever since I began playing for him. He has made me value every minute of training that I am given.

Coach Michler has influenced my approach to games in many ways. The first is I learned to concentrate on my training for the upcoming game. Making sure that I did the right things at practice leading up to the game was very important because the drills and exercises that we did were meant as preparation for the upcoming match.

Secondly, there is the mental approach. Mr. Michler taught me to make sure that I stayed calm and knew what to do before I stepped on the field, and that I was playing not only for myself, but also for my teammates and for CBC.

In addition to that my game day approach is simply this, which is quoted directly from Coach Michler, "Find a way to win." This has me prepared to do whatever I need to do to make sure that I am successful during the game and get the desired result, which is a victory.

The main things that I have learned from Coach Michler can be summed up in a number of phrases that he said to me over my four years at CBC. I will never forget them:

Score the first goal.
Start the game with high intensity.
Play like you're down 3-0.
Never let that intensity go.
Score the second goal within ten minutes while the other team is down.
Win both halves.
Play every game like it's a state championship.
Play simple.
Make plays at the right time and the right place.
Maintain continuous concentration.
Play with pride.
Play with the will of a champion.
Be better in November than you were in September.

Coach Michler not only helped develop my soccer approach, but he forever changed my approach to living life as well. He taught me to always work to improve, never get complacent, and always do everything to the best of my ability.

He taught me to take pride in what I do because whatever I am doing it is usually a lot bigger than just me. Also, he taught me to not only make myself better, but to bring others along with me on the way.

He taught me that hard work pays off and to
working. He told me to take full responsibility
and never point my finger at someone else. He explained
pay attention to detail because it is the small things that make
difference.

Along with that, Coach Michler taught me to never back down from a challenge. He said that I should always take things head on and make sure that I am prepared when I do take them on. Most importantly, he taught me to believe in myself. He has made me believe that I can achieve anything I want as long as I am willing to work for it non-stop and to strive for the goal with every ounce of my energy.

He was great with coaching individual players because he knew everyone's strengths and weaknesses. He designed specific drills for certain players and certain positions to hone their skills and to make them improve on the ones that needed improving.

He pulled kids aside and told them what they needed to work on. He did not sugar coat anything. If you were bad at something, he told you. You knew that it wasn't to embarrass you, but because he wanted you to become the best you could be.

I have never met a man who believed more about putting everything into training so that you can get better. He preached day in and day out that you should give everything you have into practice so you can get better.

Also, when Coach Michler worked with an individual player, even though he was working with only that one person, he worked with him to make that player better personally and so that the person would be more effective in the group after his individual session was over.

He was an effective practice coach because he paid such close attention to detail. He believes down to the very core of him that practice is what makes great players and teams.

He did not let you get away with doing things the wrong way. He took notes on everything at every training session and every game. He made sure that he knew what we needed to work on every time we took the pitch. He used training to prep us for games so we were prepared for every challenge.

During games he was such an effective coach because he took notes on each half. After the first half he used his notes to tell us what we needed to work at to improve in the second half so that we could come away with a victory.

Coach Michler inspired players to do well because he reminded us of who we were (CBC) and what we were representing (the school, soccer alumni, the CBC community). He instilled in each and every player the will to win, and he knew how to get the best out of each player that was on the field.

He kept us focused and made sure that we did not get out of our game. When we did, he brought us back into our way again. Mr. Michler is the best coach a player could have.

He was so effective during the state tournament because he used everything before that, every practice, every game, and every classroom session, to prepare us for tournament time. He told us how every kid wanted to be here in that moment playing for one of the big schools, and particularly CBC. He told us how we were the ones who would decide how far we would go. He put the responsibility on us to get the job done.

Along with that, Mr. Michler created a fiery passion in each and every player to want to win the right way, which is with skill, desire, and the will to succeed. He implanted in us a driving passion to win, not to except mediocrity, and to get better after every game. He also taught us to keep our composure in high stakes games. His words were, "This is just another game. It just has a little more at stake than the others."

The first memorable moment this year came for me when our teammate Jake Bond's mom died. As a team we decided to go and support Jake at his mother's funeral service at the church. I will never forget sitting in that church and seeing the Bond family in tears, but they were not the only ones. As I looked around I began to look through the pews where our team was sitting. Everyone was in tears including myself.

This touched me personally because it made me believe right then and there that we are so much more than a CBC soccer team. We are a family and as a family we will have each other's backs. I knew right there at that moment that we were going to have a special team this season.

My second most memorable moment was the state quarter-final game. The week leading up to this match was intense! Our training sessions were great. Everyone looked sharp and very determined. There was just a sense about everything that the game was going to be a battle. We had to win that battle.

Coach Michler never stopped preaching to us how incredibly hard the game was going to be and that we needed to come prepared for whatever they threw at us. After a few days off from training, we had our first practice. It was good. We were ready to go. Then the day before the game, we had a 25-minute practice just to get some touches on the ball and to make sure that we maintained our freshness.

The next day came, and it was time for the battle. I rounded the boys up in the middle of our half and said, "Guys, we cannot give up today. If you are tired, run through it. If you're hurt and get knocked down, get up. This is going to be a battle. We have to win. No excuses. Just win. Let's do it."

The first half was intense. The ball was moving up and down the field for both teams. We would have the momentum at one point in time, and then the next thing we knew they would be screaming down the flanks on a counter attack and it would take a last ditch effort on our part to win the ball back.

When the second half started I remember gathering the boys and saying, "We can do this, guys. They are good, but we are better. Let's just keep playing our game, and the result will come. Keep fighting, keep shooting, keep the ball moving, communicate. Let's go, on 3...1..2..3..CBC!"

The second half was even more intense than the first. Again the ball was back and forth. People were getting hit hard with elbows and getting cleated, but the game went on. The score was still 0-0 with about 10 minutes to play when it happened. The unimaginable happened. They scored.

I remember the sinking feeling that shot through me. For a second I thought we were finished. I thought maybe the team was going to give up, and we would become another average CBC team. But who was I kidding? We are CBC Cadets. We never quit. I remember yelling to the boys, "Let's play now! It's just like practice! Let's do this!"

That week in training we did drills that revolved around being down 1-0 and coming back from that and winning. The minutes in the game began to shrink exceptionally fast, but we kept battling, never giving up, never quitting, and not accepting failure.

With about seven minutes remaining in the second half we were given a free kick about 10 yards on the left side of their 18-yard box. I took the free kick. I remember placing the ball and listening to the crowd begin to quiet down.

As I stood there placing the ball I remember telling myself, "This is just another free kick. No pressure. This is just like practice. Just find Sam's head. I have to do this."

I backed up to take the kick, and the crowd was completely silent. I felt as if no one was there except for me and Sam. I began my run to the ball. I hit it with a little bit of a curve, and then BOOM!! GOAAAALLLL!!!!!

Sam Carenza did it! He headed the ball into the bottom right side of their net! The crowd went ballistic! The noise was deafening!! Then the half ended.

We ran over to the bench again to prepare for overtime, which consisted of two fifteen-minute periods. We went over to Mr. Michler to hear what he had to say. I remember perfectly what he said because it was the shortest speech he had ever given us.

Coach Michler said, "Boys, this game no longer has anything to do with soccer. All it has to do with now is the WILL TO WIN. Each one of you needs to have the WILL OF A CHAMPION. Go out there and win. You have every incentive to win this game. DO NOT GIVE UP. KEEP FIGHTING. HAVE THE WILL OF A CHAMPION AND WIN!"

We returned to the pitch. The first overtime period was a battle. They came out fast and with no intention of losing the game, especially not to us. The first overtime period ended. People were tired, muscles were cramping, and there was still another overtime period to go. We knew what we had to do.

Again Coach Michler said to us, "HAVE THE WILL OF A CHAMPION. THAT'S ALL THIS IS ABOUT BOYS! FIND IT IN YOURSELVES TO WIN THIS GAME. IT'S GOING TO TAKE THE WILL OF A CHAMPION!"

There was now a heightened sense of pride and intensity coursing through my body. I knew everyone felt it. Everyone was thinking the same thing: we have to win.

The second and last overtime started. We battled, tackled left and right, found the right passes at the right time, worked together to close their plays down, and won our one-on-one situations. The game was beginning to shift in our favor.

Then with about seven minutes left in the game a ball was fed to Kyle Malle on the right flank into the corner. Kyle collected the ball and turned and began dribbling at their defender.

I began to get into a passing lane for Kyle, and then he passed it to me. The ball was on my foot.

I looked up and saw four defenders coming at me. I saw the opening behind the fourth defender and I went for it. I just took off with the ball towards the near post and the end line. Then I looked for my teammates in the box.

Right then and there I saw him. Justin Bilyeu was lurking on the top of the six-yard box waiting for the cross. I played it across, which we practiced every day, and Justin instantly became the CBC Community's hero! He did it! He buried the ball into the upper 90!

Everyone on our team sprinted after Justin. We tackled him to the ground and just screamed at the top of our lungs! Everyone was so happy! The crowd was going nuts! It was the best feeling ever! We did it. We were advancing onto the semi-finals. We showed we had the WILL OF A CHAMPION!

My third most memorable moment and the best one is the day our CBC team became STATE CHAMPIONS. I do not have much to say about this game. You just had to be there.

After the game, Coach Michler said, "Perfect. Tonight's game was perfect." While playing for Coach Michler for four years I had never heard him say that. It was the best game of my life. It went by so fast. It was so much fun. He and I always joke that we wish that game would have never ended because it was so much fun to play.

I remember meeting in the morning the day of the game, and we went over our game plan to beat our opponent, who had already beaten us twice. I remember after the meeting looking around the classroom, and everyone was saying to each other, "This is going to work. We are going to win this game tonight."

Then the game came, and we dominated. We simply dominated.

There was one difference to the game from the two previous times we played them. We were not the same team. We were now a family, a fighting unit. We were going to do whatever was necessary to win the game.

We played the match as well as we could, and to top it all off Jake Bond scored the game-winning goal. It still gives me chills thinking about it. It was a true fairytale ending. I would want it no other way.

This season's team was the best team I have ever been a part of. I love each and every one of my teammates, coaches, and fans. It was the best. To forever have the title STATE CHAMPION is just a bonus on top of it all.

I will never, ever forget that moment, but most of all I will not forget the road it took to get there. This was the best moment in my life. I am forever a state champion, a CBC Cadet, and a part of the CBC Soccer Family.

I am not sure if everyone truly knows everything about Coach Michler. They might know all the external things like him being the all-time winningest soccer coach in America or that he has won six of the seven state championships at CBC or that he has accumulated over 800 victories or that he was a professional player. These are all things people probably know.

I would like people to know that Coach Michler is more than just statistics and a soccer coach. Coach Michler is excellence. Coach Michler is what most people strive to be....perfect.

Coach Michler does not only develop great soccer teams and players. He develops young men. He develops attributes in all of us who have been mentored by him that will carry us far in life.

These attributes include never quitting, continuing to improve, practicing to get better, being humble, paying attention to details, maintaining mental strength in tough situations, and most of all, having the WILL OF A CHAMPION.

CONCLUSIONS FROM MY QUEST

This book began with a simple question,

> **How did Terry Michler make such an extraordinary group performance happen in the state championship game and could his ideas be applied by groups in the business world?**

After five months of research and interviewing more than two dozen people, I have reached the conclusion that the answer is, "Yes, Terry Michler's coaching approaches have tremendous value for business managers and their teams."

One of the greatest benefits of extraordinary success in one area of life is the knowledge that has been gained and can be used in other areas.

In studying Terry Michler three major concepts stood out for me on how to generate extraordinary group performances in any type of organization. They are:

- Prepare Completely for Success
- Build Relationships for Life
- Simplify Everything

Prepare Completely for Success

I wish you could have stepped inside Terry Michler's office with me as we discussed his approaches to building great teams. When Terry described a certain team from over a decade ago he would lean over and pull out a binder. In it were detailed notes on every game from that season.

He would then pull out his laptop computer and show me detailed Power Point diagrams that he created on each of his top seven rivals. He showed me the various formations they used and how his team would defend and attack each formation.

Along the wall of his office were dozens of books and videos on soccer coaching approaches used in different parts of the world. In the time we worked on this book together Terry read half a dozen books about the top soccer coaches in the world and wrote lengthy book reviews on each of them. He then placed his book reviews on his website.

If you want to be the premier business manager in your industry, then you need a life-long commitment to constantly improving your preparation for every conceivable situation. Not only has Terry Michler seen it all before he's constantly working to be better prepared for the next time he faces a certain situation.

Terry's passion for learning, attention to detail, and pursuit of perfection are extraordinary. His consistent desire for precision in practices and games is critical to his team's success. These are the requirements to become the winningest soccer coach in U.S. history. They are also the requirements to be one of the greatest business managers in history.

Build Relationships for Life

In conversing with current and former players, soccer coaches at CBC, opposing coaches, referees, parents, protégés, mentors, and soccer enthusiasts from around the world who turn to him for advice, it became very clear to me that Terry Michler is far more than just an extraordinary technical soccer expert.

His amazing record of wins is largely a factor of the respect he earns from everyone associated with CBC Soccer. Person after person talked about his kindness and the way he genuinely cares about other people and their success.

As you pursue greatness in your career as a business manager always keep in mind the critical importance of building life-long relationships. You might only work with a certain employee for six months, but if you treat that person with complete respect and genuinely care about his or her success you may very well make a positive impact that lasts for the rest of the person's life.

Simplify Everything

In the end this book goes back to the beginning.

In the 2009 state championship game CBC demonstrated one of the finest displays of soccer that I have ever seen at any level. It was pure and simple attacking soccer. There was no wasted effort on the part of any player. Every pass had a purpose. Every player was in total sync with each of his teammates.

The whole point of this book was to uncover the secret to producing such an extraordinary group performance. It turns out that the secret is really not a secret at all. What caused that event to happen was Terry Michler's life-long commitment to making the game of soccer as simple as possible.

To achieve lasting greatness as a business manager continually work to make the work itself as simple as possible. Search for complexity everywhere in your organization and then break the complicated parts down into the simplest and most user-friendly steps that you possibly can.

If you will do that over and over again, you will create amazing group performances and deliver extraordinary results.

Prepare completely for success, build life-long relationships, and simplify everything.

These are the keys to help you find a way to win in any industry!